S0-ARL-836

THE ALLERGY-FREE COOK

Bakes Cakes and Cookies

GLUTEN-FREE, DAIRY-FREE, EGG-FREE, SOY-FREE

Laurie Sadowski

BOOK PUBLISHING COMPANY
Summertown, Tennessee

Library of Congress Cataloging-in-Publication Data

Sadowski, Laurie.
  The allergy-free cook bakes cakes and cookies / Laurie Sadowski.
      pages cm
  Includes bibliographical references.
  ISBN 978-1-57067-291-0 (pbk.) — ISBN 978-1-57067-908-7 (e-books)
  1. Gluten-free diet.   2. Gluten-free diet—Recipes.   3. Cake.   4. Cookie.   I. Title.
  RM237.86.S232 2013
  641.5'63—dc23

                                                          2012038543

Pictured on the front cover: Chocolate Chunk–Orange Bundt Cake, 30
Pictured on the back cover: Cream-Filled Maple Leaf Cookies, 104;
Wild Blueberry Brunch Cake, 36

Disclaimer: The information in this book is not intended as medical advice, treatment, or therapy for any condition, and the information and recipes contained herein are not substitutes for treatment by a qualified health-care professional. If you have any questions about your health, please consult a physician.

Calculations for the nutritional analyses in this book are based on the average number of servings listed with the recipes and the average amount of an ingredient if a range is called for. Calculations are rounded up to the nearest gram. If two options for an ingredient are listed, the first one is used. Not included are optional ingredients and serving suggestions.

Cover photos: Andrew William Schmidt
Food styling: Liz Murray, Barbara Jefferson
Cover and interior design: John Wincek

© 2013 Laurie Sadowski

All rights reserved. No portion of this book may be reproduced by any means whatsoever, except for brief quotations in reviews, without written permission from the publisher.

Book Publishing Company
P.O. Box 99
Summertown, TN 38483
888-260-8458
bookpubco.com

ISBN: 978-1-57067-291-0

Printed in Canada

19 18 17 16 15 14 13   9 8 7 6 5 4 3 2 1

Book Publishing Company is a member of Green Press Initiative. We chose to print this title on paper with 100% postconsumer recycled content, processed without chlorine, which saves the following natural resources:

  41 trees
  1,273 pounds of solid waste
  19,021 gallons of water
  3,507 pounds of greenhouse gases
  18 million BTU of energy

For more information on Green Press Initiative, visit greenpressinitiative.org.

Environmental impact estimates were made using the Environmental Defense Fund Paper Calculator. For more information, visit papercalculator.org.

Printed on recycled paper

Contents

Preface, iv • Acknowledgments, v • Introduction, vi

PART I

Gluten Sensitivities and Food Allergies 1

Check the Allergen-Free Information for Each Recipe   2

Check Food Labels Carefully   4

Combat Cross-Contamination   5

PART II

Gluten-Free Ingredients and Tips for Success 6

Stock Up: Essential Gluten-Free Ingredients   6

Banish Common Allergens   16

Tips and Techniques   20

Store Gluten-Free Treats Properly   22

Use the Right Tools   23

PART III

The Recipes 24

CAKES   24

CUPCAKES AND MINI CAKES   58

COOKIES   80

BARS, SQUARES, AND BISCOTTI   108

PART IV

The Extras 137

Conversions   137

Glossary   140

Suppliers   144

Resources   146

About the Author   146

Index   147

Preface

In the last year, you may have noticed an influx of gluten-free, vegan, and allergy-friendly items in local supermarkets, bakeries, and restaurants. When you mention your dietary restrictions, staff and servers no longer look confused. It's about time.

It's also time for this follow-up (and perfect complement) to my previous book, *The Allergy-Free Cook Bakes Bread*, which covered the essentials for baking gluten-free breads. This book provides you with the first flood of treats: cakes, cupcakes, cookies, and bars.

Like its predecessor, this volume is designed with gluten-free folks and food-allergy sufferers in mind, providing guidance and recipes for those who are hungry to learn how to feed their bellies safely, compassionately, nutritiously, and deliciously. For people with celiac disease, it's a primer on eating gluten-free. For families living with autism or ADHD, it's a source of casein-free recipes. For those with food allergies and sensitivities, it supplies recipes that are free of common allergens, including dairy products, eggs, gluten, nightshades, soy, sulfites, and wheat. Many recipes are also free of legumes, nuts, peanuts, seeds, and yeast.

Because I'm passionate about health and nutrition, I developed these recipes using safe, wholesome, and natural ingredients. Because I love food, I also made these treats downright indulgent. Now you can bake your cake . . . and eat it too.

From one cake and cookie lover to another,

Laurie Sadowski

Acknowledgments

With each book, the list continues to grow. I'm so thankful for the kind folks at Book Publishing Company, especially Cynthia Holzapfel and Jo Stepaniak. I'm grateful to my parents for their love and support and amazing ability to eat loads of treats and never put up a fuss. Thanks to Chrissy, Mat, and X for conveniently living down the road and letting me constantly drop off goodies. Gretchen, thank you for being the most amazing foodie friend. Miranda, Amy, Diane, Tracy, Caitlin, Shiona, Kristin, Brenda, Jordanna, Michelle, Stasia, Katie, Beth, Veronica, Tina, Pam, Joy, and Laura, thank you for your feedback and help. Special gratitude goes out to the inventors of the freezer and freezer-safe containers.

To everyone I know or have ever come across in life (even if just for a few minutes), thanks for listening to me constantly talk about food. Oh, and my dearest KitchenAid mixer: I've loved you since the day I met you.

Introduction

My adventures in gluten-free baking began in 2005, when I was first diagnosed with celiac disease. Like many folks with celiac disease, gluten intolerance, or food allergies, I traveled a rough road before my diagnosis. I figured bloating, diarrhea, and stomachaches were just a part of life.

I've heard that celiac disease can be triggered by trauma, surgery, or illness, and I wonder if this was the case for me. My health declined after I had a terrible bout of mononucleosis during high school. After missing almost two months of school, being hospitalized, and taking potent painkillers and steroids, I was declared "back to normal." Except I wouldn't say I felt normal; in fact, I never felt quite the same again.

For several years I endured numerous health challenges and endless medical tests; ultimately I was diagnosed with celiac disease. Almost immediately after I adopted a very strict gluten-free diet, my health dramatically improved. I soon discovered that casein and milk protein also contributed to my health problems, so I removed dairy products from my diet. I knew I was on the right track because every time I reintroduced these items, my gut protested and I got hives, a tight chest, and unbearable brain fog. Eventually, I eliminated meat, fish, and eggs too, and embraced a whole-foods vegan diet. At last, I began to feel good; no, I began to feel great!

I've always been passionate about breads and desserts, so once I started following a completely vegan diet, I knew I wanted to create gluten- and allergy-free vegan recipes for baked goods and desserts of all kinds. This concept evolved into a plan to develop a comprehensive series of cookbooks. *The Allergy-Free Cook Bakes Bread* was the first volume, packed with recipes for fluffy breads with crispy crusts, chewy flatbreads, yeasty breakfast rolls, and must-have quick breads. *The Allergy-Free Cook Bakes Cakes and Cookies* delivers a round of treats for birthday parties, holiday entertaining, weekend brunches, and every other occasion that demands a delicious dessert.

As a fitness professional and health enthusiast, I'm committed to using whole foods and replacing refined sugar, refined flour, and unhealthful ingredients with nutritious alternatives. I believe in nourishing our bodies so we can thrive, but that doesn't mean having to give up the sweets and treats we love. The recipes in this book are absolutely as scrumptious and tantalizing as their conventional counterparts, if not more so. With *The Allergy-Free Cook Bakes Cakes and Cookies*, you can at last have those Essential Chocolate Chip Cookies (page 89) you dream about, and you'll jump for joy with every single bite.

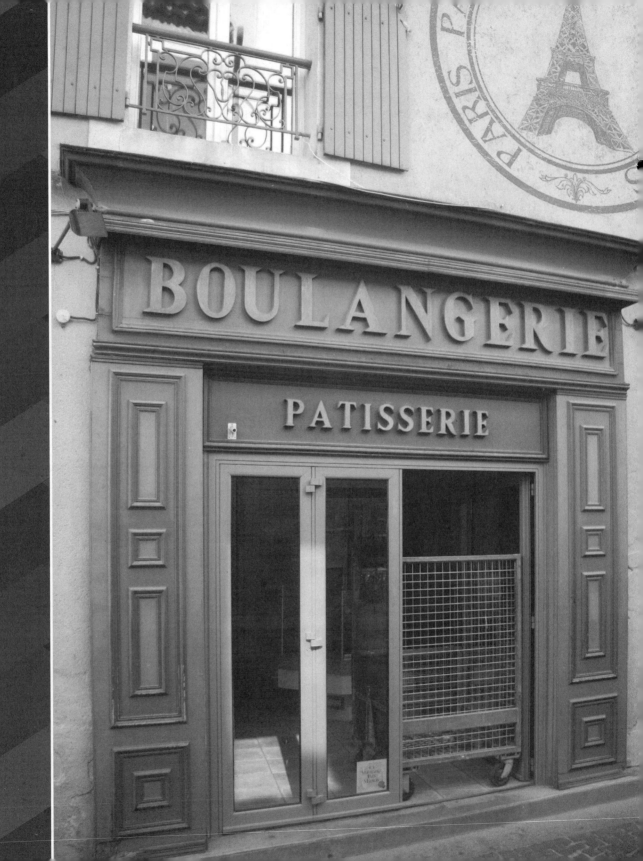

PART I

Gluten Sensitivities and Food Allergies

luten is a protein found in wheat, rye, and barley that helps bind baked goods and hold in moisture. Fittingly, the term stems from the Latin word for "glue." Gluten-containing flours, such as wheat flour, give elasticity and cohesiveness to batters, help batters to rise, and bestow a pleasing and familiar texture to the end product.

But wait a moment. If gluten performs these essential functions, does that mean baking without gluten will result in a crumbly, dry excuse of a dessert? My emphatic answer to that question is "Not at all!" I don't know about you, but I'm not too fond of excuses for dessert. That's why I wrote this book: to show you how to make delicious, texture-perfect gluten-free treats.

For many people, eating gluten isn't a problem. For others, including those with celiac disease (like me), gluten triggers debilitating symptoms, such as abdominal pain, bloating, chronic diarrhea (or constipation), neurological issues, cramping, fatigue, and weight loss (and sometimes, in adults, weight gain). Celiac disease is an autoimmune disorder that interferes with the small intestine's ability to absorb nutrients, and it can be difficult to diagnose.

Celiac disease isn't the only reason for going gluten-free. A study published in the journal *BMC Medicine* in March 2011 revealed that gluten can trigger distinct reactions in the intestines and immune system, even in people

Gluten (glü-ten):
a tenacious elastic protein substance present in cereal grains, especially wheat, that gives cohesiveness to dough.

1

who don't have celiac disease. Although it's estimated that 1 in 133 Americans have celiac disease, some experts suggest 1 in 20 Americans may have a form of gluten sensitivity or intolerance.

So if you suspect that gluten is a problem for you, it just might be, even if you've had negative test results or were told your symptoms are "all in your head." On the upside, there is a solution: adopting a lifelong gluten-free diet can heal the gut and treat celiac disease. If you're gluten intolerant, the very same tactic can help you stay symptom-free.

At first, the prospect of going gluten-free might seem overwhelming, perhaps even devastating. But you'll discover that, with a little know-how, you can enjoy a wide variety of nourishing, satisfying, tasty—and, yes, even decadent—foods, including baked goods. Ironically, adopting a gluten-free diet may be just the thing to help you realize how *many* choices you really have.

If you're new to gluten-free baking, you might find it to be a bit of a challenge: you'll have to find a way to mimic gluten—without the gluten. Believe it or not, you might find this even more of a challenge if you're a seasoned baker. This is because gluten-free baking is quite a bit different from baking with wheat, so using past knowledge won't get you very far. If you've never baked a day in your life, well, this might be your lucky day.

Sure, you may have banished good ol' all-purpose wheat flour from your pantry, but you can still choose from more than twenty varieties of gluten-free flours. Each one contributes its own superpowers to creating stellar baked goods that taste even better than those made with gluten. In addition, most of these flours are nutritionally superior to wheat flour. That's why I love using wholesome flours made from millet, quinoa, sorghum, teff, and more (see pages 6 to 8 for details on gluten-free flours). These products are increasingly available in supermarkets. If you're unable to find them locally, many online retailers sell gluten-free baking supplies (see pages 144 to 145 for supplier information).

The recipes in this book, however, are not only free of gluten. They also don't include other problematic ingredients. Because it's not uncommon for people with celiac disease or food allergies to have other food sensitivities, I clearly indicate which common allergens are absent from each recipe.

CHECK THE ALLERGEN-FREE INFORMATION FOR EACH RECIPE

 s you look through this book, you'll notice that immediately below each recipe title is a list of common allergens—including corn, grains, legumes, nuts, peanuts, seeds, and yeast—that are *not* present in the recipe.

Some allergens—such as dairy products, eggs, soy, wheat, and gluten—are never listed, because all the recipes are free of these. All recipes are also free of sulfites and nightshades. If you are sensitive to sulfites, check the labels of ingredients, such as dried fruits, that may contain sulfites.

Here is more information about items that may be listed in the allergen-free information for each recipe:

Corn. Recipes that are free of corn don't include cornmeal or cornstarch. These recipes also don't include baking powder or xanthan gum, both of which contain corn derivatives.

Grains. Recipes that are free of grains don't include any grains or "pseudo-grains." (Pseudograins are actually seeds, not grains in the classic sense, and are gluten-free. Some good examples are amaranth, buckwheat, quinoa, and wild rice.) These recipes also don't include baking powder, xanthan gum, or flours and starches made from corn, potato, or tapioca. Nut and seed flours are not grain-based.

Legumes. Recipes that are free of legumes don't include bean-based flours, such as chickpea flour (in fact, none of the recipes in this book include bean-based flours). These recipes are also free of peanuts (which are legumes, not nuts), soybeans, and soy products and derivatives. Earth Balance soy-free vegan buttery spread contains legumes (pea protein), so recipes that include vegan buttery spread are not legume-free. In addition, coconut milk and some varieties of nondairy milks contain guar gum, which is made from legumes. Recipes that include these ingredients are not marked as containing potential legume allergens, however. Be sure to check labels to find safe versions you can use.

Nuts. Recipes that are free of nuts don't include tree nuts, such as almonds, cashews, hazelnuts, pecans, and walnuts. Nuts can typically be omitted from any recipe without affecting the taste. Recipes that are free of tree nuts may include coconut, peanuts, or seeds.

Peanuts. Recipes that are free of peanuts also don't include peanut butter. Because peanuts are legumes, any recipes that contain peanuts will also contain legumes. Recipes that are peanut-free may include nuts or seeds.

Seeds. Recipes that are free of seeds don't include caraway, chia, flax, hemp, sesame, or other seeds. Recipes that are seed-free may include nuts.

Yeast. Recipes that are free of yeast also don't include cider vinegar, which is a fermented food, or vegan buttermilk, which is made with vinegar. No recipes in this book contain yeast directly.

CHECK FOOD LABELS CAREFULLY

ecause celiac disease and gluten intolerance are becoming increasingly common, food companies are now more likely to label products that contain gluten. Still, when you purchase packaged foods, be vigilant in

 Common terms for items and ingredients containing gluten, dairy, egg, or soy products

INGREDIENT	WORDS TO LOOK FOR
Wheat	Bran, bread flour, brown flour, bulgur, durum, enriched flour, farina, faro, germ, gluten, graham, groats, hydrolyzed wheat protein, Kamut, roux, seitan, semolina, spelt, triticum, udon (wheat noodles), wheat starch
Barley	Barley grass, barley groats, barley malt, barley syrup, beer, brown rice syrup (could contain barley), malt, pearl barley
Dairy/casein	All dairy products, artificial butter flavor, butter, butter oil, butterfat, buttermilk, casein, caseinates (ammonia, calcium, magnesium, potassium, sodium), cheese, cottage cheese, cream, curds, custard, ghee, goat's milk, half-and-half, hydrolysates (casein, milk protein, whey), ice milk, kefir, lactalbumin phosphate, lactate, lactic acid, lactoglobulin, lactose, lactulose, margarine, milk (condensed, dry, evaporated, malted, powdered, skim, whole), milk fat, milk protein, milk solids, nougat, pudding, rennet, sherbet, spread, whey, yogurt
Eggs	Albumin, binder, coagulant, eggs (powdered, white, whole, yolk, or yellow), emulsifier, lecithin, livetin, lysozyme, ovalbumin, ovamucin, ovamucoid, ovovitellin, vitellin
Soy	Glycerides (including diglycerides and monoglycerides), hydrolyzed proteins (plant, soy, and vegetable), lecithin, monosodium glutamate, natto, okara, soja, soy protein isolate or concentrate, textured soy flour or protein, textured vegetable protein, vegetable oil, vegetable protein, yuba
Other (check with the manufacturer)	Artificial flavors, avena (oats), bread, breading, cereal, chocolate, couscous, croutons, imitation bacon, oatmeal, oats, rye, starch

scrutinizing ingredient lists. Table 1 (opposite page) provides some guidelines on how to interpret food labels to identify "hidden" sources of gluten and other allergens, such as dairy products, eggs, and soy. If you're unsure about a product, call the food manufacturer.

COMBAT CROSS-CONTAMINATION

any foods, especially baking supplies, may be cross-contaminated with gluten. Cross-contamination can occur if gluten-free grains and gluten-containing grains are processed in the same mill or even transported in the same truck. For example, conventional oats are frequently cross-contaminated during processing, since most manufacturers also process wheat-based products on the same equipment. For that reason, people who are gluten intolerant are advised to avoid oats, and none of my recipes include oats or oat flour. (Nevertheless, if you want to use oats and oat flour, there are certified gluten-free brands available.)

The good news is that more food companies are taking a great deal of care to avoid cross-contamination. If you have any questions about a particular product, a phone call or email inquiry to the manufacturer is all that's needed to allay your concerns.

When purchasing baking ingredients, in addition to carefully checking labels, be sure to avoid the bulk section. Bins of ingredients that might otherwise be safe may have been accidentally cross-contaminated by unaware employees or shoppers.

Cross-contamination may also occur in restaurants and homes. Though the risks of dining out are obvious, you may be less aware of the dangers that lurk in your own kitchen. If other members of your household purchase foods that contain gluten, establish some guidelines regarding food storage and the use of kitchen equipment. Set aside an area exclusively for gluten-free goods and ingredients. Store gluten-containing and gluten-free baking ingredients in sealed containers in separate cabinets. Clearly mark foods and ingredients (such as condiments or baking powder) that are exclusively for gluten-free use. Finally, reserve certain appliances (such as mixers), along with porous items (such as wooden spoons and nonstick pans), for use only in gluten-free baking.

I hope these tips help you get started on the path to living gluten-free safely. As you become more comfortable with your new lifestyle, you'll find that most of these precautions become second nature.

PART II

Gluten-Free Ingredients and Tips for Success

Yes, you *can* have a generous wedge of moist carrot cake with gooey frosting (page 42), a warm-from-the-oven chocolate chip cookie (page 89), or sweet cinnamon biscotti (page 132). These treats can all be made free of gluten, dairy, eggs, soy, and other common allergens—so feel free to indulge! This chapter covers all the basics you need to know so you can start baking right away.

STOCK UP: ESSENTIAL GLUTEN-FREE INGREDIENTS

A well-stocked pantry is the key to success in gluten-free baking. After all, you don't want a craving for cake to go unanswered because all you have is a box of old baking soda and a bag of raisins, do you? Here are my favorite staples to always keep on hand.

Victory is sweetest when you've known defeat.

MALCOLM S. FORBES
PUBLISHER OF
FORBES MAGAZINE

Flours and Starches

Once upon a time, the word "flour" meant one thing: good ol' bleached all-purpose wheat flour. Today, however, we can take advantage of a variety of gluten-free flours that produce an outcome similar to—okay, *better than*—their wheat counterparts.

Gluten-free baking calls for an approach different from traditional baking. The winning formula involves combining various flours and adding a bit of xanthan gum (see page 9). Coming up with your own mixture of gluten-free flours is easy when you know the properties of each type of flour and are willing to experiment to get the taste you're looking for. Different flours have different nutritional values, and some flours perform certain tasks better than others. Each gluten-free flour has its own unique taste and texture, but never judge a recipe by sampling the raw batter. Some gluten-free flours have a strong and sometimes even bitter taste before they are baked.

I encourage you to adapt my recipes by substituting your own gluten-free flour combinations or using a store-bought mix. A number of suppliers sell packaged gluten-free flour blends, but I prefer to make my own for a few reasons. First, I like to try a variety of flour combinations in different baked goods. Second, most commercial blends contain a large proportion of rice flour and an excessive amount of starch, a combination that lacks nutrition. Third, commercial blends often contain gelatin or powdered milk, both of which are animal derived. So read labels carefully before buying a ready-made blend.

Here's a list of the gluten-free flours and starches I use in my cake and cookie recipes. For ideas about substituting other gluten-free flours and starches, see sidebar (page 9).

Sorghum flour. Smoother than most flours and high in protein, sorghum flour is a component in many packaged gluten-free flour blends. It has a slight molasses flavor and is rich in nutrients. Sorghum flour is one of my favorites; I like its taste and texture, and I also appreciate its low cost.

Millet flour. Millet flour is slightly sweet and imparts a moist, tender crumb to baked goods, which is why I love it for cakes. It's also rich in B vitamins.

Quinoa flour. Quinoa flour adds protein and nutrients to gluten-free recipes. It has a very distinct flavor and can generally be substituted with amaranth, bean, or millet flour.

Teff flour. High in protein, slightly sweet, and somewhat nutty, teff flour is another one of my favorites. It's the main ingredient in the fermented Ethiopian bread *injera* and also works well in recipes that call for cocoa.

Tapioca flour. Also known as tapioca starch, tapioca flour is made from the cassava plant and is suitable for baking and thickening. It adds moistness and gives baked goods a tender, chewy texture.

TABLE 2 Nutritional content and weight of gluten-free flours

Flour (¼ cup)	Calories, kcal	Fat, grams	Fiber, grams	Protein, grams	Weight, grams
Almond flour	160	14	3	6	28
Amaranth flour	110	2	3	4	30
Arrowroot starch	110	0	1	0	32
Buckwheat flour	100	1	4	4	30
Chickpea flour	110	2	5	6	30
Coconut flour	120	3	12	4	28
Cornmeal	110	1	5	2	32
Cornstarch	120	0	0	0	32
Fava bean flour	110	0.5	8	9	33
Garfava flour	150	2.5	3	9	30
Hazelnut flour	180	17	3	4	28
Millet flour	110	1	4	3	30
Potato flour	160	1	3	4	45
Potato starch	160	0	0	0	48
Quinoa flour	120	2	4	4	28
Rice flour, brown	140	1	2	3	39.5
Rice flour, sweet white	180	0.5	1	3	51
Rice flour, white	150	0.5	1	2	39.5
Sorghum flour	120	1	3	4	31.75
Tapioca flour	100	0	0	0	30
Teff flour	113	1	4	4	30

Arrowroot starch. Also known as arrowroot flour, arrowroot starch provides structure and lightness when paired with high-fat or high-protein gluten-free flours.

Cornstarch. A fine, powdery thickening agent made from corn, cornstarch has no flavor and is typically combined with various flours in gluten-free baking.

Cornmeal. Coarser than corn flour, cornmeal may be white, yellow, or blue, depending on the corn it's made from. The featured ingredient in cornbread, cornmeal provides a dense, crumbly texture.

Substituting Flours and Starches

For the best results when substituting flours, replace one flour for another that has the same weight and a similar protein content. Amaranth flour and buckwheat flour, for example, interchange well because their protein content is comparable and they weigh the same per cup. See table 2 (opposite page) for the nutritional content and weight of gluten-free flours. Note that because each gluten-free flour has a different weight, it's not always possible to substitute measure for measure.

To substitute wheat flour in a conventional recipe, combine a lower-protein gluten-free flour with a higher-protein gluten-free flour, include a starch for balance, and add xanthan gum (below) to hold everything together. Ideally, the weight of the gluten-free flour should match the weight of the wheat flour in the original recipe. See table 3 (page 10) for the nutritional content and weight of wheat flours to help you determine which gluten-free flours to substitute.

Xanthan Gum

If you're new to gluten-free baking, xanthan gum may seem mysterious. In fact, this essential ingredient *is* a bit magical, giving baked goods a gluten-like consistency, without a speck of gluten. A little bit of xanthan gum goes a long way, taking over the role of gluten and holding the other ingredients together.

Xanthan gum is made from corn; if your diet is corn-free, try guar gum, which is made from legumes, instead. An equal amount of guar gum can replace xanthan gum in most cases, though this can require a bit of trial and error. Note that guar gum can cause gastrointestinal issues in some people.

Different types of baked goods require different amounts of xanthan gum. For cakes, muffins, cookies, and bars, use ½ teaspoon of xanthan gum per 1 cup of gluten-free flour.

Leavening

Baking powder and baking soda are indispensable ingredients in baking, particularly in recipes that contain no gluten or eggs. Without them, batters and doughs may fail to bind and cakes and cookies may become flat, dense, or dry. When a recipe calls for both baking powder and baking soda, the baking powder does the majority of the leavening, while the baking soda adds tenderness.

Baking powder. Baking powder is a chemical leavening agent that helps batters rise and, in eggless baking, also assists in binding the ingredients. Using

TABLE 3	Nutritional content and weight of wheat flours				
Flour (¼ cup)	Calories, kcal	Fat, grams	Fiber, grams	Protein, grams	Weight, grams
Wheat flour (all-purpose)	120	1	1	4	34
Wheat flour (whole wheat)	110	0.5	4	4	33

too much baking powder can cause a bitter taste or make baked goods collapse; using too little will inhibit rising or make baked goods tough. Baking powder contains cornstarch. If you're allergic or sensitive to corn, you can replace each teaspoon of baking powder with the following combination: ½ teaspoon of cream of tartar, ¼ teaspoon of baking soda, and ¼ teaspoon of potato starch.

Baking soda. Also known as sodium bicarbonate, baking soda is a chemical leavener that is about four times stronger than baking powder. It's used in recipes that contain an acid, such as citrus juice, molasses, vegan buttermilk (see sidebar, page 17), or vinegar. Baking soda begins to react as soon as it's mixed with wet ingredients, so be sure to bake the item immediately after mixing the batter. Using too much baking soda will result in a coarse, dry crumb or soapy taste.

Testing Baking Powder and Baking Soda for Freshness

Using fresh baking powder and baking soda is a must.

- To test baking powder, mix 1 teaspoon with ½ cup of hot water; fresh baking powder will begin to bubble immediately.

- To test baking soda, mix ¼ teaspoon with 2 teaspoons of vinegar; fresh baking soda will begin to bubble immediately.

Sweeteners

Sweeteners are essential ingredients in any dessert or treat, but that doesn't mean we can't be choosy about the types we use. For my recipes, I choose minimally processed sweeteners that have nothing artificial added.

Agave nectar. Made from the agave plant, agave nectar is a liquid that is naturally sweeter than sugar and has a lower glycemic index than other sweeteners. It has a neutral flavor and is available in light, amber, and raw varieties.

Confectioners' sugar. Also known as powdered sugar or icing sugar, confectioners' sugar is a granulated sugar that has been ground to a powder and combined with cornstarch to prevent clumping or crystallization. It's most often used in frostings and glazes or for adding aesthetic appeal when sifted over cakes just before serving. Some brands are ground with wheat starch, so be sure to check labels.

Dates. Fiber-rich dates add a natural sweetness to treats. In some of my recipes, dates are the only sugar source. I use and prefer honey dates (see pages 144 to 145 for supplier information). If the dates you have aren't tender, soak them in warm water for 10 minutes before using. Note that some manufacturers may dust their dates with flour before packaging.

Molasses. Molasses is a thick syrup that is separated from raw cane sugar during the sugar-making process. Its distinct taste is most often associated with gingerbread. Light molasses comes from the first boiling of the sugar syrup and has a light flavor and color. Dark molasses comes from the second boiling and has a deeper flavor and color. Blackstrap molasses comes from the third boiling; it's rich in iron and has an intense flavor.

Pure maple syrup. Not to be confused with pancake syrup, pure maple syrup is made from the sap of maple trees. In general, there are two broad classifications of maple syrup: grade A (also called "grade 1," "extra light," or "light") and grade B (also called "grade 2," "amber," or "dark amber"). I recommend grade B for its stronger maple flavor.

Pure maple sugar. Maple sugar remains when the sap that is used to make maple syrup is boiled until all the moisture has evaporated.

Unrefined cane sugar. Most of my recipes call for unrefined cane sugar. As its name indicates, unrefined cane sugar is minimally processed, which leaves minerals, trace elements, and vitamins intact. Unrefined cane sugar imparts the same sweetness as refined sugar, with a hint of molasses flavor that adds depth to baked goods. I prefer Sucanat, the brand made by Wholesome Sweeteners.

Other common sweeteners include refined granulated white sugar, brown sugar, demerara sugar, stevia, and brown rice syrup. (Check labels before using these sweeteners; brown rice syrup, in particular, may contain gluten.) If you use any of these sweeteners in my recipes, results may vary. For example, baked goods may lack body or turn out sweeter (or less sweet) than intended.

To use a liquid sweetener in place of a granulated sweetener, use ⅔ cup of liquid sweetener for every cup of granulated sweetener and decrease the other liquids in the recipe by 2 tablespoons. When using agave nectar, decrease the oven temperature by 25 degrees F and increase the baking time by 5 to 10 minutes.

Fats

Fats are essential ingredients that provide the necessary texture, flavor, and mouthfeel to baked goods. Although the amount of fat used in a recipe can be decreased, omitting the fat completely often results in undesirably heavy or chewy baked goods. Common fat options include olive oil, coconut oil, canola oil, and vegan buttery spread. See page 18 for the 411 on these items.

Nondairy Milks

There are plenty of nondairy milks to choose from, and every time I go to the grocery store I seem to find yet another new variety. For baking, I prefer to use unsweetened almond milk in either vanilla or original flavors. Other common varieties include soy milk and rice milk. Nondairy milks made from hempseeds, potatoes, hazelnuts, coconut, and even quinoa are also available. Not all nondairy milks are gluten-free, however, so be sure to check the label and ingredient list before purchasing.

Nuts, Seeds, and Nut and Seed Butters

Nuts and seeds add texture, flavor, healthful fats, fiber, and protein to desserts and treats. For extra flavor, use toasted nuts (see sidebar, opposite page). Homemade nut and seed butters (see sidebar, opposite page) are easy to make and offer the same advantages as nuts and seeds. If you prefer to purchase nut and seed butters, including tahini, look for all-natural varieties. Preferably, the only ingredient should be the nut itself. Roasted nut and seed butters have a pronounced flavor, while raw versions are subtler in taste.

When opening a new jar of nut butter or seed butter, stir in the natural oil that separates out and rises to the top. If you pour off the oil, the butter will be hard and dry instead of creamy and spreadable.

Toasting Nuts, Seeds, and Coconut

To toast nuts, seeds, or shredded dried coconut in the oven, spread in a single layer on a baking pan. Preheat the oven to 400 degrees F and bake for 7 to 8 minutes, until golden, shaking the pan a few times. To toast in a skillet, spread in a single layer. Cook over medium-high heat, stirring often, for 5 to 7 minutes, until golden. Toasted nuts and seeds should be fragrant and just a shade or two darker than the raw nuts or seeds. They burn quickly, so pay close attention and remove them from the pan immediately.

Super Seeds

You might not think that tiny seeds can add extra oomph in baking, but they certainly do. Chia seeds and ground flaxseeds not only provide essential omega-3 fatty acids, but they also work wonderfully as binders in place of eggs. For more information on egg substitutes, see table 5 (page 20).

Making Homemade Nut and Seed Butters

To make homemade nut or seed butter, put about 3 cups of nuts or seeds in a food processor or high-speed blender. Process the nuts or seeds until they resemble graham cracker crumbs. Stop the food processor occasionally to scrape down the work bowl with a rubber spatula. Continue to process until the nuts or seeds come together in a ball. If desired, add a pinch of salt. Continue to process until completely smooth and the mixture turns into a paste, stopping the food processor occasionally to scrape down the work bowl if necessary.

Homemade nut butters made from oilier nuts (such as macadamia nuts) may be thinner than other butters but should become firm when refrigerated. If you're having trouble getting a completely smooth finish, add 1 to 2 tablespoons of a nut-based or neutral-tasting oil. Nut and seed butters can be made with raw or roasted nuts or seeds.

Coconut

When I was younger, I didn't like the overly sweet cakes and cookies that contained sugary strands of coconut. Now, however, I appreciate the many ways that coconut-based ingredients can enhance baked goods. For example, coconut oil (see page 18) gives a tender, moist crumb to cakes.

Coconut butter. It's simple to prepare homemade coconut butter, which tastes better and is more affordable than commercial varieties. To make coconut butter, follow the instructions for making homemade nut and seed butters (see sidebar, page 13), using 4 cups of unsweetened finely shredded dried coconut and 2 to 3 tablespoons of melted coconut oil. Coconut butter will become firm as it stands.

Full-fat canned coconut milk. Canned coconut milk has a smooth, luxurious taste and works beautifully in baking. When refrigerated for at least 12 hours, cans of full-fat coconut milk produce coconut cream, which is a must-have replacement for heavy cream or whipping cream. Carefully open the can without shaking or tipping it and use a spoon to scrape out the hardened cream at the top. To make whipped cream using the cream from full-fat coconut milk, see page 51.

Shredded dried coconut. I prefer to use unsweetened finely shredded dried coconut in baking (see pages 144 to 145 for supplier information). If you use sweetened coconut, you may want to decrease the sugar called for in the recipe.

Fruit and Fruit Purées

In some baked goods, fruit is the star ingredient. For example, bananas are the headliners in Banana-Chai Cupcakes (page 68) and apples shine in Autumn Apple Cake with Cider Sauce (page 52).

Citrus zest and juice. The zest and juice of lemons, limes, and oranges add punch to baked goods and can highlight and complement many other flavors.

Dried fruits. Raisins, cherries, cranberries, apricots, and dates are versatile and tasty additions to many recipes. Look for all-natural, sulfite-free, and preservative-free versions, and check the label to ensure they aren't dusted with flour.

Fruit purées. Sometimes fruit purées can be used to replace eggs or fat, adding a new texture and flavor. See table 5 (page 20) for egg substitutes and pages 17 to 19 for fat replacements.

Extracts

Extracts add a lot of flavor. Basic extracts (such as vanilla, almond, mint, and maple) should be pantry staples, while specialty extracts (such as chocolate, coconut, orange, lemon, and hazelnut) can add interest to certain recipes. A little extract goes a long way, and this small amount of liquid won't disrupt the balance of wet and dry ingredients.

Spices and Salt

Where would we be without ginger for our gingerbread? Spices please the palate, and I love pumping up the flavor of baked goods with them.

Salt does more than just add saltiness and bring out the flavor of other ingredients. It also gives structure to batters and doughs, slows down chemical reactions for more even baking, and extends the finished product's shelf life. Salt comes in several forms, including fine, coarse, sea, and kosher. I prefer to use fine sea salt in my recipes. Truth be told, my favorite flavor combination is salty and sweet.

Cereal

Although I typically avoid using prepackaged foods in my kitchen creations, I occasionally make exceptions. For example, some cereals can be more than part of a balanced breakfast when they are used to create wholesome baked goods.

Buckwheat cereal. Also called creamy buckwheat cereal, this stone-ground cereal is made from coarsely ground raw buckwheat groats (not kasha, which is toasted). It's available from Bob's Red Mill, labeled as "Creamy Buckwheat" (see pages 144 to 145 for supplier information and details about this product's gluten-free status).

Flaked cereal. Canadian Nanaimo Bars (page 112) call for a flaked cereal, and I recommend Mesa Sunrise by Nature's Path, both for its nutritional value and texture.

Crispy rice cereal. Some varieties of crispy rice cereal aren't gluten-free because they contain barley malt. Other varieties contain preservatives, such as BHT. The version by Nature's Path is made from brown rice and is free of refined sugars and preservatives.

Cocoa and Chocolate

The allure of the almighty cocoa bean is evident in its scientific name, *Theobroma cacao*, which literally means "food of the gods." I concur. Cocoa powder works great (and by great, I mean amazing) for most baking tasks. When choosing other forms of chocolate, such as chips or chunks, be aware that traces of milk can be found in some brands, so check labels carefully if dairy products are a concern for you.

Cocoa powder. There are two types of unsweetened cocoa powder: natural and Dutch-processed. Natural cocoa powder is very bitter and has a deep chocolate flavor. It reacts with baking soda to create leavening action. Dutch-processed cocoa powder is treated with an alkali to neutralize cocoa's natural acidity. It's milder than natural cocoa powder and has a rich but delicate flavor. To replace Dutch-processed cocoa with natural cocoa (or vice versa), see the sidebar below.

When making frostings and fillings, you can also use raw cacao powder, which is cocoa in its most unadulterated state. Raw cacao powder provides just a hint of natural sweetness.

Semisweet chocolate chips and chunks. A number of recipes in this book call for nondairy semisweet chocolate chips or chunks. Semisweet chocolate contains 35 percent cocoa solids and delivers just the right amount of sweetness. I recommend Enjoy Life brand semisweet mini chocolate chips and chunks because they are guaranteed allergen-free (see pages 144 to 145 for supplier information).

Other varieties of chocolate include dark chocolate, milk chocolate, and white chocolate. None of the recipes in this book use these ingredients, which may be cross-contaminated with gluten, dairy, or other allergens.

Interchanging Dutch-Processed and Natural Cocoa

It's easy to substitute one kind of cocoa for the other.

- For every 3 tablespoons of Dutch-processed cocoa powder called for in a recipe, use 3 tablespoons of natural cocoa powder plus ⅛ teaspoon of baking soda.

- For every 3 tablespoons of natural cocoa called for in a recipe, use 3 tablespoons of Dutch-processed cocoa powder plus ⅛ teaspoon of cider vinegar or lemon juice.

Cider Vinegar

Cider vinegar, also called apple cider vinegar, is the magic ingredient in many gluten-free and egg-free baked goods. Because it's an acid, cider vinegar reacts with baking soda, causing batters to rise. Gluten-free and egg-free batters can easily lack the "lift" found in traditional baked goods, and adding a little vinegar contributes to a good rise and tenderness. Cider vinegar can also be combined with a nondairy milk to make vegan buttermilk (see sidebar, page 17).

BANISH COMMON ALLERGENS

nce you've found alternatives to gluten, it's time to focus on replacements for other common allergens, such as dairy products, eggs, and soy.

Instead of Milk

There are many nondairy milks. The trick is knowing which ones work well for different types of baked goods. Each has its own properties, flavor, and ideal uses.

Canned coconut milk. A little thicker than other nondairy milks, canned coconut milk works well in baking. The lite varieties are very creamy and tasty alternatives to the full-fat versions (and, in most cases, work just as well, and no one will ever miss the fat). Full-fat coconut milk produces a moist, flavorful texture to baked goods and can be substituted for heavy cream in most recipes (see page 14). Note that coconut milk in the carton is designed for drinking (rather than cooking and baking), and the recipes in this book do not use this type of coconut milk.

Nut and seed milks. Because of their naturally sweet and nutty flavor, nut and seed milks are ideal for desserts and treats. The consistency and flavor of unsweetened almond milk makes it my favorite for baking.

Rice milk. Naturally sweet, rice milk works well for baking, although it has a much thinner consistency than most other nondairy milks. Rice milk isn't used in the recipes in this book.

Soy milk. Available in many flavors, soy milk works well in baking. Note, however, that baked goods made with soy milk brown more quickly than those made with other nondairy milks. Soy milk isn't used in the recipes in this book.

Making Vegan Buttermilk

I use the term "vegan buttermilk" in my recipes when I want to provide a nondairy alternative to this classic baking ingredient. Dairy-based buttermilk is milk that has been cultured, increasing the milk's acidity and causing it to clump together and thicken. To make vegan buttermilk, put 1 tablespoon of cider vinegar in a liquid measuring cup. Pour in as much unsweetened nondairy milk as needed to equal the total amount of buttermilk called for in the recipe. Stir and let stand for 10 minutes. Use nut milk, seed milk, or soy milk for the best results.

Instead of Butter

Like milk, butter can be easily replaced in dairy-free baking. Reliable staples like vegan buttery spread or oil will do the trick in most instances. For certain applications, applesauce, avocado, or nut and seed butters can be used.

Vegan buttery spread. Buttery-tasting vegan spread is sold in tubs or sticks and can be used measure for measure instead of butter in any recipe. I recommend the Earth Balance brand. When shopping for vegan buttery spread, opt for one that is nonhydrogenated and free of trans fats. Also be sure to check labels to avoid hidden dairy and soy ingredients (see table 1, page 14). Note that Earth Balance's soy-free version includes legumes (pea protein).

Canola and olive oils. Canola and olive oils are economical and work well when a buttery taste isn't necessary. See table 4 (below) for how to substitute oil for butter. When buying oils, choose cold-pressed varieties that have been produced at low heat to maintain flavor, nutritional value, and color.

Coconut oil. Coconut oil is a nonhydrogenated source of healthful saturated fats, and it's my favorite oil for baking. There are two kinds of coconut oil: virgin (or unrefined) and refined (or simply not labeled virgin). Virgin coconut oil has the distinct scent of coconut and costs about twice as much as the refined version. Despite the cost difference, refined coconut oil offers the same health benefits as virgin coconut oil. When purchasing refined coconut oil, look for a high-quality brand made by a company that also produces virgin coconut oil.

At room temperature (unless your house is very warm), coconut oil will be the texture of softened butter, ideal for beating into a batter. Coconut oil is liquid when warmed and rock solid when stored in the refrigerator. If a recipe

TABLE 4	Substituting oil for butter or margarine
BUTTER OR MARGARINE	**OIL**
1 teaspoon	¾ teaspoon
1 tablespoon	2½ teaspoons
2 tablespoons	4½ teaspoons
¼ cup	3 tablespoons
⅓ cup	¼ cup
½ cup	6 tablespoons
⅔ cup	½ cup
¾ cup	9 tablespoons
1 cup	¾ cup

calls for softened coconut oil, it should be room temperature and soft enough to scoop, but not melted. Using melted coconut oil may alter the consistency of the batter or dough.

Applesauce. Using applesauce can significantly decrease the amount of fat in a recipe but can result in a slightly denser baked good. Avoid the chewy texture of fat-free baked goods by replacing only 2 to 3 tablespoons of the fat called for with applesauce.

Avocado. Mashed avocado flesh works well as an alternative for buttery spread or oil because it has a naturally buttery flavor, is high in fat, and can replace buttery spread or oil measure for measure. However, because avocado can change the texture and color of baked goods, use it as a replacement for only half of the fat called for.

Nut and seed butters. When you add nut or seed butters to a recipe, you may be able to decrease the amount of oil or vegan buttery spread and create a new texture and taste. Nut and seed butters do double duty, because they work as binding agents too. Replace one-quarter to one-half of the fat called for with a nut or seed butter.

Instead of Eggs

There are a variety of ways to replace eggs in recipes, but not all alternatives offer the same outcome. Select an egg substitute based on the egg's task in a given recipe. If you're replacing the egg in a conventional recipe, start with a recipe that requires only one or two eggs. Table 5 (page 20) provides all the details you need. Note that in conventional recipes, two egg whites are equivalent to one egg.

Instead of Soy

Although all of the recipes in this book are free of soy and don't include any form of soy, such as tofu or vegan cream cheese, it's very important to check the labels of the products you're using for hidden sources of soy (see table 1, page 4). Be sure to check labels of vegan buttery spread for soy-free versions or experiment with oil instead (see table 4, opposite page). As noted, some soy-free varieties include legumes. I recommend Earth Balance brand for baking because it consistently gives positive results and imparts a buttery flavor. When buying nondairy milk and nondairy semisweet chocolate chips, check to make sure they are soy-free (soy lecithin is a common ingredient). Almond Breeze and Enjoy Life make options that are allergy-friendly and soy-free.

TABLE 5 — Common egg substitutes and their uses

SUBSTITUTE FOR 1 EGG	BEST USED IN	PURPOSE	NOTES
3 tablespoons warm water whisked with 1 tablespoon ground flaxseeds or chia seeds; let stand until thickened	Breads, cakes, most cookies, muffins, scones	Binder	• Adds fiber and good fats • Adds a bit of a nutty taste • Use golden flaxseeds to avoid brown specks in light-colored baked goods • Can create a gummy texture
1½ teaspoons powdered egg replacer mixed with 2 tablespoons warm water	Some cookies, hard icings	Leavener	• Neutral taste • Good for use in baked goods in which ground flaxseeds would be apparent and unattractive
¼ cup puréed silken tofu	Brownies, heavy loaves, pound cake	Binder, moisturizer	• Adds moisture and density
¼ cup mashed or puréed fruit (such as applesauce, avocado, bananas, or pumpkin) plus ¼ teaspoon baking powder	Breads, cakes, cupcakes, muffins	Moisturizer	• Adds moisture and density • For 2 eggs, use ½ cup fruit plus only ¼ teaspoon baking powder
2 to 3 tablespoons nut or seed butter	Bars, brownies, muffins	Binder	• Adds density and flavor
1 to 3 tablespoons cornstarch, arrowroot starch, or tapioca flour	Puddings, sauces, bar toppings	Thickener	• Start with 1 tablespoon and add more until desired thickness is achieved
3 to 4 tablespoons nondairy milk plus ¼ teaspoon baking powder	Breads, cakes, cupcakes, muffins	Moisturizer	• Adds moisture • For 2 eggs, use 6 to 8 tablespoons nondairy milk plus only ¼ teaspoon baking powder

TIPS AND TECHNIQUES

I f you have *The Allergy-Free Cook Bakes Bread*, you already know that gluten-free yeast dough doesn't look or behave like wheat-based dough. Similarly, you'll find that gluten-free cake batters are thicker than their conventional counterparts. On the other hand, gluten-free cookie dough looks and feels much like its gluten-containing counterpart, but it certainly won't taste the same when raw. So be warned: if you love snacking on cookie dough before it's baked, you might notice an unpleasant bitterness from the raw gluten-free flours.

When making the recipes in this book or adapting your favorites, refer to these tips and techniques for the best results. In addition, always be sure to read the recipe thoroughly before you begin. Though it sounds obvious, it's important to read a recipe several times before starting so you have an idea of the steps involved (do you have all the necessary equipment?) and you're less likely to forget an ingredient (oops—there aren't any nuts in the pantry!). Finally, be sure to read the introductions to each recipe section, where you'll find even more helpful tips.

Ingredients

Make sure ingredients are at the right temperature. Use ingredients that are at room temperature, unless the recipe states otherwise.

Check expiration dates. Avoid using out-of-date or stale ingredients. Gluten-free flours, nuts, and seeds can go rancid, so if you don't use them up quickly, it's a good idea to store these ingredients in the freezer. Other items, such as spices, can lose their potency, and baking powder and baking soda can lose their effectiveness.

Choose fruits in season. Whenever possible, prepare fruit-based recipes when the fruits are in season. By opting for fresh, ripe, seasonal fruits, you can often use less sweetener because the fruits will be at their peak of flavor and sweetness.

Equipment

Preheat the oven longer than you think is necessary. After about five minutes, most ovens will indicate that they are preheated. The truth, however, is that many ovens take much longer to fully reach the temperature they're set at, so always allow fifteen minutes for the oven to preheat.

Line the baking pans. Because gluten-free dough can be sticky, make it a rule to line baking sheets or pans with parchment paper, aluminum foil, or silicone baking mats (see page 140), unless the recipe specifies otherwise. Plus, lining the pans allows for easier cleanup.

Techniques

Measure carefully. Accuracy is critical to success in baking, so take your time when measuring each ingredient.

Spoon and level. Use the spoon-and-level method for measuring flours. Here's how: stir the flour in its container just before using to aerate it, spoon the flour into the measuring cup, and level off the flour with the straight edge (non-cutting edge) of a table knife. It's especially important to use this method when making cakes and cupcakes; cookies and bars are a little more forgiving.

Combine dry ingredients thoroughly. Always use a dry whisk to combine dry ingredients, such as flour, leavener, starch, and xanthan gum, before combining them with wet ingredients. This step will ensure that the dry mixture is aerated and the ingredients are evenly distributed.

Toast nuts and seeds. Toasting nuts and seeds adds extra flavor to baked goods (see sidebar, page 13).

Adjust baking times when using frozen fruit. If a recipe calls for fruit and you choose frozen fruit rather than fresh, the batter will be colder and the baking time will need to be longer.

Watch for browning. Gluten-free baked goods tend to brown more quickly than conventional baked goods because of the higher protein and fat content of the flours. Baked goods containing agave nectar and soy milk also tend to brown faster. If you find that baked goods are browning too quickly, use aluminum foil to tent the pan and continue to bake until the items are cooked through.

Test for doneness. To test cakes and cupcakes for doneness, insert a toothpick in the center. If the toothpick comes out clean, the item is done. If any wet batter clings to the toothpick, more baking is required. In addition to using the toothpick test, you can gently press the middle of the cake with your fingers; if the cake springs back, it's done. The cake will also begin to pull away from the sides of the pan. Most cookies and bars are done when golden or starting to brown around the edges. Check each recipe for specific information on how to test for doneness.

STORE GLUTEN-FREE TREATS PROPERLY

Most gluten-free treats stay fresh at room temperature or will keep in the refrigerator for a few days, but some are best enjoyed the day they are made. For example, cookies may lose crispness or frostings may melt. For these reasons, I provide storage recommendations with each recipe. Freezing leftovers is a good idea; that way you can have a sweet treat on hand whenever a craving strikes. Midnight snack, anyone?

Before storing desserts, whether at room temperature, in the refrigerator, or in the freezer, be sure to let them cool completely first. Once they're cool, slice them in portions (if appropriate), then wrap them tightly in plastic before storing in a ziplock bag or container.

Generally, cakes, cupcakes, cookies, bars, and frostings will keep in the freezer for three months. Note that freezing may affect the texture, but it certainly won't affect the taste.

USE THE RIGHT TOOLS

Just as it is important to stock the right ingredients for baking, it is also essential to have the right kitchen tools. The columns in table 6 (below) include my recommendations for the items you absolutely need along with those that are helpful to have on hand.

TABLE 6 Kitchen tools and accessories

MUST-HAVES	HELPFUL ITEMS
Aluminized steel baking pans and sheets (heavy-duty commercial-grade)	Blender or immersion blender (for easy puréeing)
Cooling racks	Cake caddy (for conveniently transporting and storing cakes and cupcakes)
Cookie cutters of all shapes and sizes	Coffee grinder (for grinding nuts, seeds, and whole spices)
Cutting boards (at least 2)	Fine grater, such as Microplane (for citrus zests and fresh ginger)
Oven mitts	Kitchen timer (use in addition to an oven timer when baking two things at once or when cooling one item and baking another)
Food processor (for making nut butters, puréeing, and chopping)	Oil spray bottles
Kitchen scissors and knives (chef's knife, serrated knife, and paring knife)	Pastry bags, dessert decorating tool, or large ziplock bags with a bottom corner snipped off for piping frosting
Measuring cups (wet and dry), measuring spoons, mixing bowls, silicone spatulas, slotted spoons, toothpicks, wire whisks, wooden spoons, sifter or sieve (for sifting cocoa powder, confectioners' sugar, and flour)	Pastry mat (plastic work surface with labeled inches and rounds; handy for rolling dough or using as a nonstick surface)
Pan liners, such as parchment or silicone baking mats (see page 140)	Scale for weighing flours for adapting conventional recipes
Rolling pin	Hand mixer (for thinner batters or frosting)
Stand mixer	First aid, such as an aloe vera plant for skin burns

PART III

The Recipes

Cakes

Vegetables are a must on a diet. I suggest carrot cake, zucchini bread, and pumpkin pie.

JIM DAVIS, CARTOONIST, *GARFIELD*

See Loaded Carrot Cake, page 42, and Chocolate Carrot Cake, page 44.

What I love most about cakes is their versatility. A simple cake that features one dominant flavor and a light sprinkling of confectioners' sugar is the perfect accompaniment to morning coffee or weekend brunch. But dress that cake up, and it transforms into a decadent dessert. I'm all for going the extra step to make a cake just *that* much more spectacular—after all, who wouldn't enjoy a moist layer cake filled with thick fudge and topped with a luscious buttercream frosting? No one in their right mind, that's who.

Whether you need a wholesome everyday treat or a tantalizing centerpiece for a celebratory meal, I've got it covered in this chapter. Each recipe features specific details for preparing, baking, and storing cakes. For the best results, read the following general tips before you dive into the recipes.

TIPS FOR MAKING GREAT CAKES

Ingredients

- Use ingredients that are at room temperature. This may require advance planning if you store gluten-free flours in the freezer or refrigerator.

- Where instructed, combine the dry and wet ingredients in three steps. Here's how: Combine about one-third of the flour mixture and one-half of the liquid and mix well. Add another one-third of the flour mixture and the remaining liquid and mix well. Then add the remaining flour mixture and mix just until all the ingredients are combined.

Equipment

- To prepare the cake pan, first coat it with vegan buttery spread or a neutral-tasting oil (use a paper cupcake liner or paper towel to do the dirty work). Then sprinkle it with sorghum flour or, if you're making chocolate cake, unsweetened cocoa powder. Use about 1 tablespoon of flour per pan, gently shaking and tilting the pan until the inside is covered with a fine coating. Tap out and discard any excess flour.

- Alternatively, line the bottom of the pan with parchment paper. First oil the pan, then insert a piece of parchment paper that has been cut to fit (trace the bottom of the cake pan on the parchment paper before cutting it, then use scissors to cut the parchment paper just slightly inside the lines). Lightly oil the parchment paper as well.

TABLE 7 Troubleshooting when baking cakes

PROBLEM	POSSIBLE CAUSES AND SOLUTIONS
The cake fell.	• The batter contained too much liquid or too little flour. • The cake was underbaked. • The oven door was opened during the first half of the baking time. • The oven temperature was set too low or set incorrectly.
The cake didn't rise.	• The batter wasn't mixed well. • The batter contained too little leavening. • The leavening wasn't fresh (see sidebar, page 10, for how to test for fresh leavening).
The cake has a crusty exterior.	• Dark nonstick bakeware was used. • The cake was overbaked. • The oven was too hot (invest in an oven thermometer if you want to be sure the oven is at the right temperature).
The cake is dry.	• The batter contained too much leavening. • The batter didn't contain enough liquid. • The oven temperature was set too low.
The cake's surface is cracked or holey.	• The batter contained too much flour. • The batter contained too little leavening. • The oven was too hot.
The cake is gummy or dense (but isn't supposed to be).	• The baking was done in a humid climate or at a high altitude. • The oven was too hot. • The leavening wasn't fresh (see sidebar, page 10, for how to test for fresh leavening).

- Decrease the oven temperature by 25 degrees F if using a dark nonstick baking pan or glass baking dish. These pans may cause cakes to bake and brown more quickly.

- Mix cake batters using the equipment specified in each recipe. Electric mixers work well for beating gluten-free cake batters, which are often a little thicker than wheat batters. Some gluten-free cake batters, however, are better mixed by hand.

- Use a metal offset spatula or the back of a large spoon to spread the cake batter in the prepared pan. An offset spatula has a stiff metal blade that bends slightly at the handle. Its angled shape allows you to spread the batter easily and evenly inside the pan. It also works well for frosting cakes and cupcakes.

Measuring

- Use the spoon-and-level method (see page 21) for measuring flours and starches. Don't use a measuring cup to scoop the flour, or you will get too much flour and end up with a dry or heavy cake.

- For even baking and rising, fill the cake pan no more than one-half to two-thirds full.

- To ensure that cake layers are the same thickness, use an equal amount of batter in each cake pan. If possible, use a kitchen scale to weigh the pans after filling them; if you don't have a scale, insert a toothpick or the tip of a knife in the middle of the batter to measure and compare the approximate height of the batter in each pan.

Baking

- Bake cakes in the center of the oven. If there are two or more pans, leave at least one inch of space between the pans and the sides of the oven for proper heat circulation.

- Don't open the oven door until it's time to check the cake for doneness. The cool air will affect the rising, especially during the first half of the baking time.

- Check for doneness after the minimum baking time has elapsed. The baking times in my recipes are given as ranges to allow for variations in conditions.

- Triple-check for doneness by using three different methods to ensure the cake is baked through. First, insert a toothpick in the center of the cake. It should come out clean. Second, check to see that the cake is pulling away from the sides of the pans and the top is lightly browned. Third, press the middle of the cake with your fingers. If the indentation springs back, the cake is done; if the indentation remains, the cake needs to bake for one or two more minutes.

Cooling, Slicing, and Storing

- Cool the cake in the pan for ten minutes before removing it, unless instructed otherwise. Let the cake cool on a wire rack—not on top of a hot oven.

- If the cake sticks to the pan, put a clean towel in the sink and pour boiling water over the towel. Put the cake pan on the hot towel and let it stand for three minutes. The cake should then come out of the pan easily.

- To cut crumb-free slices, heat a knife by dipping it in very hot water and wipe it dry before slicing.
- To keep cake fresh, wrap it with a slice of fresh apple and store it in a sealed container.

TECHNIQUES FOR FROSTING AND FILLING CAKES

- Frost the cake only when it's completely cool.
- To keep the cake from moving while you're frosting it, put a dab of frosting between the cake and the serving dish or cake stand.
- When making a layer cake, spread the frosting or filling over the top of the bottom layer, then cover it with the next layer, pressing down lightly.
- Use a metal offset spatula to frost the cake without any frills. For a smooth, finished look, heat a metal offset spatula by dipping it in hot water and wiping it dry before running it over the frosting.

- Use the back of a spoon to create pretty, decorative swirls on top of the cake.
- For a little more panache, use a cake-decorating bag or kit.
- For a crumb-free finish, spread a thin layer of frosting over the top and sides of the cake. Refrigerate the cake for fifteen minutes to harden the frosting. Then spread a thicker layer of frosting on top of this smooth base.
- To make a quick and delicious frosting, put a sealed bag of nondairy semisweet chocolate chips in very hot water and let it stand until the chocolate chips are melted. Remove the bag from the water and pat it dry. Use your hands to gently press on the bag until the chocolate feels smooth. Snip off a corner of the bag and squeeze the melted chocolate over cooled cakes or cupcakes.

Mixing and Matching Cakes and Frostings

Most of my recipes include multiple components, such as a recipe for the cake or cupcake, a recipe for the filling, and a recipe for the frosting, glaze, or other topping. Feel free to mix and match the cakes and frostings to suit your tastes and creative urges. Following is a list of the most versatile frostings and glazes. Others, not included here, are best served with the cake or cupcake they were designed for. Note that if you want to use a frosting that is included as part of a cupcake recipe to frost a layer cake or Bundt cake, you'll need to double the frosting recipe.

- Bakery-Style White Frosting (page 67)
- Banana Frosting (page 69)
- Cashew Butter Buttercream Frosting (page 63)
- Chocolate Buttercream Frosting (page 39)
- Chocolate Frosting (page 64)
- Chocolate Ganache (page 31)
- Chocolate Glaze (page 37)
- Chocolate-Macadamia Frosting (page 64)
- Coconut Cream Frosting (page 43)
- Good-for-You Frosting (page 45)
- Maple Buttercream Frosting (page 105)
- Maple Syrup Glaze (page 71)
- Orange Glaze (page 65)
- Peanut Butter Buttercream Frosting (page 35)
- Thick Vanilla Frosting (page 75)
- Toasted Coconut Glaze (page 78)
- Whipped Cream (page 51)

I often find my thoughts drifting to this cake, which tastes sinful even though it's really not. I long for its **melt-in-your-mouth** tenderness, silky ganache, and citrusy tang. For the **best flavor,** use freshly squeezed orange juice.

CHOCOLATE CHUNK-ORANGE Bundt Cake

FREE OF: LEGUMES,* NUTS, PEANUTS   YIELD: 12 SLICES

CHOCOLATE CHUNK–ORANGE CAKE

1¼ cups sorghum flour, plus more for sprinkling the pan

1 cup millet flour

½ cup plus 1 tablespoon tapioca flour

¼ cup arrowroot starch

2 teaspoons baking powder

1½ teaspoons xanthan gum

1 teaspoon baking soda

1 teaspoon fine sea salt

1½ cups unrefined cane sugar

⅔ cup coconut oil, melted

¼ cup finely grated orange zest (about 4 large oranges)

¼ cup freshly squeezed orange juice

1 tablespoon ground flaxseeds

2 teaspoons vanilla extract

1¾ cups vegan buttermilk (see sidebar, page 17)

1½ cups nondairy semisweet chocolate chunks or chips

1 tablespoon cider vinegar

To make the cake, preheat the oven to 350 degrees F. Lightly oil a 10-inch (12-cup) Bundt pan, using a pastry brush to thoroughly coat the bottom and sides of the pan. Sprinkle with sorghum flour, tapping out the excess.

Put the sorghum flour, millet flour, ½ cup of the tapioca flour, and the arrowroot starch, baking powder, xanthan gum, baking soda, and salt in a large bowl. Stir with a dry whisk until combined.

Put the sugar, coconut oil, orange zest, orange juice, flaxseeds, and vanilla extract in the bowl of a stand mixer, with the paddle attachment, or a large bowl. Turn the stand mixer or a hand mixer on medium-low speed. Beat until well combined.

Turn the mixer to low speed. Alternately add the flour mixture (in three additions) and the vegan buttermilk (in two additions), beginning and ending with the flour mixture, beating well after each addition. Turn off the mixer.

Put the chocolate chunks and remaining 1 tablespoon of tapioca flour in a small bowl. Toss until the chunks are well coated. Add the chunks to the batter, stirring with a rubber spatula until evenly distributed. Immediately stir in the cider vinegar until just combined.

Scrape the batter into the prepared pan using the rubber spatula. Smooth the top with the spatula. Bake in the center of the oven for 40 to 45 minutes, until a toothpick inserted in the center of the cake comes out clean. The cake will be golden brown, begin to pull away from the sides of the pan, and will spring back when lightly touched.

Let cool in the pan for 10 minutes, then invert the cake directly onto a serving dish. Let cool to room temperature before you prepare the drizzle and ganache.

Per slice: 525 calories, 5 g protein, 26 g fat (19 g sat), 77 g carbs, 360 mg sodium, 137 mg calcium, 6 g fiber

ORANGE DRIZZLE

½ cup confectioners' sugar, sifted

½ teaspoon finely grated orange zest

2 tablespoons freshly squeezed orange juice, plus more as needed

¼ teaspoon vanilla extract

CHOCOLATE GANACHE

2 tablespoons nondairy milk

1½ teaspoons coconut oil or vegan buttery spread (*for legume-free, use coconut oil)

¼ cup nondairy semisweet chocolate chips

To make the drizzle, put the confectioners' sugar in a small bowl. Stir in the orange zest, orange juice, and vanilla extract until smooth. Stir in up to 1 tablespoon additional orange juice, 1 teaspoon at a time, as needed to achieve a runny consistency.

To make the ganache, put the nondairy milk and coconut oil in a small saucepan. Warm over medium heat just until the coconut oil is melted. Immediately remove from the heat and stir in the chocolate chips until they are melted and the mixture is smooth.

Spoon the drizzle and ganache over the cake, letting them run down the sides. (The drizzle and ganache can be applied alternately or the ganache can be applied after the drizzle.) Serve at room temperature.

Stored in a sealed container, the cake will keep for 3 days at room temperature or 2 months in the freezer.

If you love the combination of coffee and caramel, *you'll adore this moist Bundt cake. It's brimming with coffeehouse flavor.*

Caramel-Macchiato BUNDT CAKE

FREE OF: NUTS, PEANUTS   YIELD: 12 SLICES

ESPRESSO CAKE

1 cup strongly brewed coffee, at room temperature (see tip, page 39)

3 single-serve packets extra-bold instant coffee (see tip)

1¼ cups sorghum flour, plus more for sprinkling the pan

1 cup millet flour

½ cup tapioca flour

¼ cup arrowroot starch

2 teaspoons baking powder

1½ teaspoons xanthan gum

1 teaspoon baking soda

½ teaspoon fine sea salt

1¾ cups unrefined cane sugar

⅔ cup coconut oil, melted

1 tablespoon ground flaxseeds

2 teaspoons vanilla extract

1 cup vegan buttermilk (see sidebar, page 17)

1 tablespoon cider vinegar

To make the cake, preheat the oven to 350 degrees F. Lightly oil a 10-inch (12-cup) Bundt pan, using a pastry brush to thoroughly coat the bottom and sides of the pan. Sprinkle with sorghum flour, tapping out the excess.

Pour the brewed coffee into a small bowl. Stir the instant coffee into the brewed coffee until dissolved.

Put the sorghum flour, millet flour, tapioca flour, arrowroot starch, baking powder, xanthan gum, baking soda, and salt in a large bowl. Stir with a dry whisk until combined.

Put the sugar, coconut oil, flaxseeds, and vanilla extract in the bowl of a stand mixer, with the paddle attachment, or a large bowl. Turn the stand mixer or a hand mixer on medium-low speed. Beat until well combined. Add the coffee mixture. Beat until well combined.

Turn the mixer to low speed. Alternately add the flour mixture (in three additions) and the vegan buttermilk (in two additions), beginning and ending with the flour mixture, beating well after each addition. Turn off the mixer. Add the vinegar and briskly stir with a rubber spatula until just combined.

Scrape the batter into the prepared pan using the rubber spatula. Smooth the top with the spatula. Bake in the center of the oven for 45 to 50 minutes, until a toothpick inserted in the center of the cake comes out clean. The cake will be golden brown, begin to pull away from the sides of the pan, and will spring back when lightly touched.

Let cool in the pan for 10 minutes, then invert the cake directly onto a serving dish. Let cool to room temperature before you prepare the glaze.

Per slice: 451 calories, 3 g protein, 17 g fat (13 g sat), 75 g carbs, 388 mg sodium, 76 mg calcium, 3 g fiber

CARAMEL-COFFEE GLAZE

6 tablespoons unrefined cane sugar

¼ cup nondairy milk

¼ cup vegan buttery spread

3 tablespoons strongly brewed coffee

½ teaspoon fine sea salt

½ teaspoon vanilla extract

1½ cups confectioners' sugar, sifted

COFFEE GARNISH

2 teaspoons finely ground coffee beans (not instant coffee)

To make the glaze, put the sugar, nondairy milk, vegan buttery spread, and coffee in a small saucepan. Bring to a boil over high heat. Boil for 2 minutes, whisking constantly. Immediately remove from the heat and stir in the salt and vanilla extract. Let cool for 5 minutes, then whisk in the confectioners' sugar until smooth.

Reserve about ½ cup of the glaze for serving, and spoon the remaining glaze over the cake, letting it run down the sides.

To garnish, put the finely ground coffee in a wire sieve and shake it evenly over the top of the cake. Serve immediately or at room temperature, spooning some of the reserved glaze over each slice.

Stored in a sealed container, the cake will keep for 3 days at room temperature or 2 months in the freezer.

TIPS

- Because some instant coffee varieties are not gluten-free or free of other allergens, I recommend using an extra-bold variety of Starbucks VIA Ready Brew (I like the Italian Roast). For the cake, start by using three single-serve packets. To ramp up the coffee flavor even more, use four packets.

- If you love the combination of chocolate and coffee, apply the ganache from the Chocolate Chunk–Orange Bundt Cake (page 31) before sprinkling this cake with the coffee garnish.

- For even more chocolate decadence, put ¾ cup of nondairy semisweet chocolate chips in a small bowl. Add 1 tablespoon of tapioca flour and toss until the chips are well coated. Add the chocolate chips to the batter before adding the vinegar, stirring with a rubber spatula until evenly distributed.

I love the combination of **chocolate and peanut butter,** and I've discovered that people of all ages seem to concur. If you know any of these chocolate–peanut butter lovers, here's a tip: make their birthdays happy with this decadent cake, which virtually explodes with their **favorite flavors.**

CHOCOLATE-PEANUT BUTTER Explosion

FREE OF: NUTS, SEEDS

YIELD: 12 SLICES

PEANUT BUTTER CAKE

- 1¼ cups sorghum flour, plus more for sprinkling the pans
- ½ cup quinoa flour
- ½ cup arrowroot starch
- 2 teaspoons baking powder
- 1½ teaspoons xanthan gum
- ½ teaspoon baking soda
- ¼ teaspoon fine sea salt
- 1¼ cup unrefined cane sugar
- ½ cup plus 2 tablespoons creamy natural peanut butter (see tip)
- 2 tablespoons vegan buttery spread
- ⅓ cup unsweetened apple- sauce
- 2 teaspoons cider vinegar
- 2 teaspoons vanilla extract
- 1 cup nondairy milk, plus more as needed

To make the cake, preheat the oven to 350 degrees F. Lightly oil two 9-inch round baking pans. Sprinkle with sorghum flour, tapping out the excess.

Put the sorghum flour, quinoa flour, arrowroot starch, baking powder, xanthan gum, baking soda, and salt in a medium bowl. Stir with a dry whisk until combined.

Put the sugar, peanut butter, and vegan buttery spread in the bowl of a stand mixer, with the paddle attachment, or a large bowl. Turn the mixer or a hand mixer on medium-high speed. Beat until creamy and smooth. Add the applesauce, vinegar, and vanilla extract. Continue to beat until well combined, about 2 minutes, occasionally stopping to scrape down the bowl with a rubber spatula if necessary.

Turn the mixer to low speed. Alternately add the flour mixture (in three additions) and the nondairy milk (in two additions), beginning and ending with the flour mixture, beating well after each addition. Turn off the mixer. The mixture should be thick, but if it's extremely thick and looks dry, add up to ¼ cup additional nondairy milk, 1 tablespoon at a time, to create a thick, smooth batter.

Scrape the batter into the prepared pans using the rubber spatula. Smooth the tops using the spatula. Bake in the center of the oven for 25 to 30 minutes, until a toothpick inserted in the center of each cake comes out clean. The cakes will be golden brown, begin to pull away from the sides of the pans, and will spring back when lightly touched.

Let cool in the pans for 5 minutes. Carefully remove the cakes from the pans and put them on a cooling rack. Let cool to room temperature.

To make the filling, put the chocolate chips, peanut butter, nondairy milk, and salt in a medium saucepan. Warm over medium heat, stirring constantly, until the chocolate chips have melted. Immediately remove from the heat and stir in the confectioners' sugar until smooth. Transfer to a small bowl and refrigerate for 15 minutes.

Per slice: 567 calories, 12 g protein, 27 g fat (7 g sat), 75 g carbs, 240 mg sodium, 102 mg calcium, 5 g fiber

CHOCOLATE–PEANUT BUTTER TRUFFLE FILLING

¾ cup nondairy semisweet chocolate chips, melted

⅓ cup creamy natural peanut butter (see tip)

¼ cup nondairy milk

⅛ teaspoon fine sea salt

½ cup confectioners' sugar, sifted

PEANUT BUTTER BUTTERCREAM FROSTING

½ cup creamy natural peanut butter (see tip)

¼ cup vegan buttery spread, softened

1 teaspoon vanilla extract

1½ cups confectioners' sugar, sifted

2 tablespoons nondairy milk, plus more as needed

CHOCOLATE GANACHE

2 tablespoons nondairy milk

1½ teaspoons vegan buttery spread

¼ cup nondairy semisweet chocolate chips

Line one of the 9-inch round pans with parchment paper (to reuse the parchment paper that was used to bake the cake, simply turn it over). Scrape the filling into the pan using a rubber spatula and spread it evenly to about ¾ inch from the sides of the pan. Smooth the top with the spatula. Refrigerate until firm, about 45 minutes.

To make the frosting, put the peanut butter, vegan buttery spread, and vanilla extract in the bowl of a stand mixer, with the paddle attachment, or a large bowl. Turn the mixer or a hand mixer to medium-high speed. Beat until fluffy and smooth, about 5 minutes. Turn the mixer to low speed. Add ¾ cup of the confectioners' sugar and the nondairy milk. Beat until well combined. Beat in the remaining confectioners' sugar, adding up to 2 tablespoons additional nondairy milk, 1 tablespoon at a time, until the frosting is smooth and spreadable.

To make the ganache, put the nondairy milk and vegan buttery spread in a small saucepan. Warm over medium heat just until the vegan buttery spread is melted. Immediately remove from the heat and stir in the chocolate chips until they are melted and the mixture is smooth.

To assemble the cake, carefully transfer one layer to a serving dish or cake stand. Invert the filling onto your hand, then put it on the layer and peel off the parchment paper. (It should come off easily; if it sticks, refrigerate the filling until it's no longer sticky.) Cover with the other layer, pressing down lightly. Spread the frosting over the top and sides of the cake using a metal offset spatula. Spoon the ganache over the top and sides of the cake, letting it run down the sides.

Let the cake stand until the ganache is set, about 10 minutes. Serve immediately or keep at room temperature until serving time. The peanut butter flavor in the cake will become more pronounced as the cake stands.

Stored in a sealed container, the cake will keep for 2 days at room temperature or 2 months in the freezer. Wrapped tightly in plastic wrap and stored in a sealed container, individual cake layers will keep for 2 days at room temperature or 2 months in the freezer.

TIPS

- Because different brands of natural peanut butter vary in consistency, you may need to adjust the amounts of other ingredients in the cake batter, filling, and frosting to compensate. The cake batter should be very thick but spreadable; if it isn't spreadable, add more nondairy milk. I have found that I usually need to add 1 to 2 tablespoons of additional nondairy milk to the cake batter. For the filling and frosting, you may need to add more confectioners' sugar.

- To make a bittersweet ganache, stir in 2 tablespoons of unsweetened cocoa powder and 1 tablespoon of additional nondairy milk after adding the chocolate chips.

Boston Cream Pie is a bit of a misnomer. In fact, this delectable "pie" is made from layer cakes. Fluffy and light, with just the right amount of moist crumb, the layers are the perfect complement to the thick custard filling and chocolaty glaze.

BOSTON Cream Pie

FREE OF: NUTS, PEANUTS   YIELD: 12 SLICES

CUSTARD FILLING
(prepare at least 2 hours in advance)

1½ cups nondairy milk

¼ cup light agave nectar

¼ cup cornstarch

2 tablespoons sorghum flour

⅛ teaspoon fine sea salt

2 teaspoons vanilla extract

BASIC TWO-LAYER CAKE

1¼ cups sorghum flour

1 cup millet flour

½ cup tapioca flour

¼ cup arrowroot starch

2 teaspoons baking powder

2 teaspoons xanthan gum

1 teaspoon baking soda

1 teaspoon fine sea salt

6 tablespoons warm water

2 tablespoons ground flaxseeds

½ cup vegan buttery spread

¼ cup coconut oil, softened
    (see page 18)

1½ cups unrefined cane sugar

2 teaspoons vanilla extract

1¼ cups plus 2 tablespoons
    vegan buttermilk (see
    sidebar, page 17)

1 tablespoon cider vinegar

To make the custard filling, put ¼ cup of the nondairy milk and the agave nectar, cornstarch, sorghum flour, and salt in a small bowl. Whisk until completely smooth.

Pour the remaining 1¼ cups of nondairy milk into a small saucepan. Bring to a simmer over medium heat, then immediately remove from the heat. Pour about ¼ cup of the warm nondairy milk into the agave nectar mixture and whisk until well combined. (This step will help eliminate any lumps in the custard). Whisk the agave nectar mixture into the warm nondairy milk in the saucepan. Cook over medium-low heat, whisking constantly, until thickened, about 2 minutes. Once the mixture is very thick, whisk briskly for 30 seconds longer and immediately remove from the heat. Stir in the vanilla extract. Scrape the custard into a small bowl using a rubber spatula. Put a piece of waxed paper or plastic wrap directly on top of the custard, pressing gently so it sticks to the top. Let cool to room temperature, then refrigerate for at least 2 hours or for up to 2 days.

To make the cake, preheat the oven to 350 degrees F. Lightly oil two 9-inch round baking pans, line them with parchment paper, and lightly oil the parchment paper.

Put the sorghum flour, millet flour, tapioca flour, arrowroot starch, baking powder, xanthan gum, baking soda, and salt in a medium bowl. Stir with a dry whisk until combined.

Put the water in a small bowl or measuring cup. Stir in the flaxseeds and let stand until thickened, about 5 minutes. Put the vegan buttery spread and oil in the bowl of a stand mixer, with the paddle attachment, or a large bowl. Turn the mixer or a hand mixer on medium-high speed. Beat for 4 minutes. Add the sugar and beat for 4 to 5 more minutes, until well combined and fluffy. Add the flaxseed mixture and vanilla extract. Continue to beat until well combined, about 2 minutes, occasionally stopping to scrape down the sides of the bowl with a rubber spatula if necessary.

Per slice: 470 calories, 5 g protein, 21 g fat (10 g sat), 71 g carbs, 164 mg sodium, 170 mg calcium, 5 g fiber

CHOCOLATE GLAZE

⅓ cup nondairy milk

Heaping 1 cup nondairy semisweet chocolate chips

Turn the mixer to low speed. Alternately add the flour mixture (in three additions) and vegan buttermilk (in two additions), beginning and ending with the flour mixture, beating well after each addition. Turn off the mixer. Add the vinegar and briskly stir with a rubber spatula until just combined.

Scrape the batter into the prepared pans using the rubber spatula. Smooth the tops with the spatula. Bake in the center of the oven for 25 to 30 minutes, until a toothpick inserted in the center of each cake comes out clean. The cakes will be golden brown, begin to pull away from the sides of the pans, and will spring back when lightly touched.

Let cool in the pans for 10 minutes. Carefully remove the cakes from the pans and put them on a cooling rack. Let cool to room temperature before filling with the custard and topping with the glaze.

To make the glaze, put the nondairy milk in a small saucepan. Bring to a boil over medium heat. Immediately remove from the heat and stir in the chocolate chips until they are melted and the glaze is smooth.

To assemble the cake, carefully transfer one layer to a serving dish or cake stand. Spread the filling evenly over the top of the layer using a metal offset spatula. Cover with the other layer, pressing down lightly. Spoon the glaze over the top and sides of the cake, letting it run down the sides. Let stand for about 30 minutes, until the glaze has cooled. Serve at room temperature.

Stored in a sealed container, the cake will keep for 2 days at room temperature or in the refrigerator. Wrapped tightly in plastic wrap and stored in a sealed container, individual cake layers will keep for 2 days at room temperature or 2 months in the freezer.

TIP: The custard filling can be served on its own. For a sweeter custard, add up to 2 tablespoons additional agave nectar to taste.

VARIATION: This basic two-layer cake recipe (minus the custard filling and glaze) just begs to be dressed up with your favorite frostings, fillings, and toppings for birthdays and other celebrations. For a classic combination, pair it with Bakery-Style White Frosting (page 67), Chocolate Buttercream Frosting (page 39), or my favorite, Chocolate-Macadamia Frosting (page 64).

Chocolate cake rocks my world, especially when it features moist layers, a **silky mousse** filling, and a classic chocolate **buttercream** frosting.

Triple-Chocolate LAYER CAKE

FREE OF: LEGUMES,* NUTS, PEANUTS, SEEDS   YIELD: 12 SLICES

CHOCOLATE MOUSSE FILLING
(prepare at least 12 hours in advance)

4 small ripe avocados, at room temperature (see tips)

¾ cup unsweetened cocoa powder

½ cup light agave nectar

2 tablespoons coconut oil, melted

2 teaspoons vanilla extract

⅛ teaspoon fine sea salt

CHOCOLATE CAKE

1¼ cups sorghum flour

¾ cup unsweetened cocoa powder, plus more for sprinkling the pans

½ cup teff flour

½ cup arrowroot starch

¼ cup tapioca flour

2 teaspoons baking soda

1½ teaspoons xanthan gum

½ teaspoon baking powder

¼ teaspoon fine sea salt

2 cups unrefined cane sugar

1 cup brewed coffee, warm or cool (see tip)

1 cup cold water

6 tablespoons coconut oil, melted

2 tablespoons cider vinegar

2 teaspoons vanilla extract

To make the filling, remove the flesh from the avocados. Put the avocado flesh, cocoa powder, agave nectar, coconut oil, vanilla extract, and salt in a food processor. Process until smooth. Refrigerate for at least 12 hours (see tip).

To make the cake, preheat the oven to 350 degrees F. Lightly oil two 9-inch round baking pans. Sprinkle with cocoa powder, tapping out the excess.

Put the sorghum flour, cocoa powder, teff flour, arrowroot starch, tapioca flour, baking soda, xanthan gum, baking powder, and salt in a large bowl. Stir with a dry whisk until combined.

Put the sugar, coffee, water, coconut oil, vinegar, and vanilla extract in a medium bowl. Stir briskly with a whisk until well combined.

Make a well in the center of the flour mixture. Pour the sugar mixture into the well and stir until well combined using a rubber spatula. The batter will be thinner than most gluten-free cake batters.

Scrape the batter into the prepared pans using the rubber spatula. Smooth the tops with the spatula. Bake in the center of the oven for 25 to 30 minutes, until a toothpick inserted in the center of each cake comes out clean. The cakes will begin to pull away from the sides of the pans.

Let cool in the pans for 10 minutes. Carefully remove the cakes from the pans and put them on a cooling rack. Let cool to room temperature before you prepare the frosting.

To make the frosting, put the vegan buttery spread in the bowl of a stand mixer, with the paddle attachment, or a large bowl. Turn the stand mixer or a hand mixer on medium-high speed. Beat until the vegan buttery spread is fluffy and smooth, about 3 minutes. Turn the mixer to low speed. Add the cocoa

Per slice: 606 calories, 4 g protein, 22 g fat (12 g sat), 97 g carbs, 444 mg sodium, 32 mg calcium, 6 g fiber

CHOCOLATE BUTTERCREAM FROSTING

½ cup vegan buttery spread

¾ cup unsweetened cocoa powder, sifted

4 tablespoons nondairy milk, plus more as needed

1 tablespoon vanilla extract

2⅔ cups confectioners' sugar, sifted

To make this recipe legume-free, use Chocolate Frosting (page 64) or Good-for-You Frosting (page 45) instead of the Chocolate Buttercream Frosting.

powder, 2 tablespoons of the nondairy milk, and the vanilla extract. Beat until well combined. Add 1 cup of the confectioners' sugar. Beat until smooth after each addition. Alternately add the remaining confectioners' sugar and remaining nondairy milk, beating until smooth. If the frosting seems dry, add up to 1 tablespoon additional nondairy milk, 1 teaspoon at a time, until thick and spreadable. Turn the mixer to high speed and beat until creamy and fluffy, 4 to 5 minutes.

To assemble the cake, carefully transfer one layer to a serving dish or cake stand. Spread the filling evenly over the top of the layer using a metal offset spatula. Cover with the other layer, pressing down lightly. Spread the frosting over the top and sides of the cake using the metal offset spatula. Serve immediately or refrigerate for up to 2 hours before serving.

Stored in a sealed container, the cake will keep for 2 days at room temperature or 2 months in the freezer. Wrapped tightly in plastic wrap and stored in a sealed container, individual cake layers will keep for 2 days at room temperature or 2 months in the freezer.

TIPS

- For the best results, make the Chocolate Mousse Filling at least one day in advance to allow the avocado flavor to mellow and the chocolate to really shine.

- It's important to bring the avocados to room temperature before making the filling. If you combine cold avocado flesh with the other filling ingredients, the coconut oil will solidify and there will be chunks of solid fat in the filling.

- When making recipes that call for coffee, it can be convenient to have a French coffee press. This affordable piece of equipment prepares good coffee in minutes, saving you the hassle of making a whole pot. You can purchase a French coffee press for under $15 at most coffee shops and home stores.

The flavors of fall unite in this moist, light pumpkin cake, which has a tart cranberry filling, a crunchy pecan topping, and a sweet maple glaze. This dessert comes together quickly and makes for a great ending to any harvest dinner. Thanksgiving, anyone?

Pumpkin Cake WITH CRANBERRY FILLING AND PECAN STREUSEL

FREE OF: LEGUMES, PEANUTS, SEEDS   YIELD: 12 SLICES

PECAN STREUSEL TOPPING

Heaping ½ cup chopped pecans

3 tablespoons unrefined cane sugar

2 tablespoons sorghum flour

¾ teaspoon ground cinnamon

1 tablespoon canola oil

PUMPKIN CAKE

1 cup sorghum flour, plus more for sprinkling the pans

¾ cup teff flour

½ cup tapioca flour

2½ teaspoons ground cinnamon

2 teaspoons baking powder

1½ teaspoons ground ginger

1 teaspoon xanthan gum

1 teaspoon baking soda

¾ teaspoon fine sea salt

½ teaspoon ground nutmeg

1 cup plus 2 tablespoons mashed cooked or canned pumpkin (not pie filling; see tip)

6 tablespoons coconut oil, melted

1½ cups unrefined cane sugar

1 cup nondairy milk

1 tablespoon vanilla extract

2 tablespoons cider vinegar

To make the topping, put the pecans, sugar, sorghum flour, and cinnamon in a small bowl. Mix to combine. Stir in the canola oil until the mixture sticks together.

To make the cake, preheat the oven to 350 degrees F. Lightly oil two 9-inch round baking pans. Sprinkle with sorghum flour, tapping out the excess.

Put the sorghum flour, teff flour, tapioca flour, cinnamon, baking powder, ginger, xanthan gum, baking soda, salt, and nutmeg in a large bowl. Stir with a dry whisk until combined.

Put the pumpkin and coconut oil in a medium bowl. Use the whisk to mix until combined. Whisk in the sugar until well blended. Whisk in the nondairy milk and vanilla extract until dark and creamy, about 2 minutes.

Make a well in the center of the flour mixture. Pour the pumpkin mixture into the well and stir until combined using a rubber spatula. Add 1 tablespoon of the vinegar and briskly stir with the rubber spatula until just combined. Add the remaining tablespoon of vinegar and briskly stir until just combined.

Scrape the batter into the prepared pans using the rubber spatula. Smooth the tops with the rubber spatula. Sprinkle the topping on one of the cakes. Bake both cakes in the center of the oven for 25 to 30 minutes, until a toothpick inserted in the center of each cake comes out clean. The cakes will be golden brown, begin to pull away from the sides of the pans, and will spring back when lightly touched. The cake with the topping may need to bake for 1 to 2 minutes longer than the one without the topping.

Let cool in the pans for 15 minutes. Carefully remove the cakes from the pans and put them on a cooling rack. Let cool to room temperature before you prepare the filling and glaze.

Per slice: 371 calories, 3 g protein, 13 g fat (7 g sat), 65 g carbs, 307 mg sodium, 93 mg calcium, 5 g fiber

CRANBERRY FILLING

2½ cups fresh or frozen cranberries

1 tablespoon finely grated orange zest (about 1 orange)

¼ cup freshly squeezed orange juice or apple cider

4 tablespoons light agave nectar, plus more as needed

2 teaspoons cornstarch

MAPLE GLAZE

½ cup confectioners' sugar, sifted

2 teaspoons maple extract

1 teaspoon nondairy milk, plus more as needed

To make the filling, put the cranberries, orange zest, and 2 tablespoons of the orange juice in a medium saucepan over medium heat. Cook, stirring often, until the cranberries begin to pop, about 8 minutes. Add the agave nectar and mix well.

Put the remaining orange juice in a small bowl. Whisk in the cornstarch. Stir the cornstarch mixture into the cranberry mixture. Mix well. Cook for 1 additional minute, until the filling has thickened. Remove from the heat. Let cool for 5 minutes. Taste for sweetness—be careful, the filling will be very hot. Stir in up to 2 more tablespoons of agave nectar, 1 tablespoon at a time, to taste. Scrape the filling into a medium bowl using a rubber spatula. Refrigerate until the filling is very thick but still warm, about 15 minutes.

To make the glaze, put the confectioners' sugar in a small bowl. Stir in the maple extract and 1 teaspoon of the nondairy milk until smooth. Stir in up to 1 teaspoon additional nondairy milk as needed to achieve a runny consistency.

To assemble the cake, carefully transfer the cake layer without the topping to a serving dish or cake stand. Spread the filling evenly over the top of the layer using a metal offset spatula. Cover with the other layer, topping-side up, pressing down lightly. Spoon the glaze over the top of the cake, letting it run down the sides. Serve slightly warm or at room temperature. The flavors will become more pronounced as the cake stands.

Stored in a sealed container, the cake will keep for 3 days at room temperature or 2 months in the freezer. Wrapped tightly in plastic wrap and stored in a sealed container, individual cake layers will keep for 3 days at room temperature or 2 months in the freezer.

TIPS

- Save time by making the filling while the cake is baking. Although the filling can still be warm when you serve the cake, be sure it has cooled enough to thicken. If the filling is made in advance and stored in the refrigerator, bring it to room temperature before using.

- The consistency of the batter will vary depending on whether fresh or canned pumpkin is used. Similarly, different brands of canned pumpkin will produce different results. The batter should be thick but spreadable. If it's too difficult to spread, stir in 1 additional tablespoon of nondairy milk.

If you prefer carrot cake that is loaded with goodies, this one's for you. It's packed with plump raisins, toasted walnuts, and juicy pineapple, then slathered with a creamy coconut frosting.

LOADED CARROT CAKE WITH Coconut Cream Frosting

FREE OF: LEGUMES, NUTS,* PEANUTS, YEAST   YIELD: 12 SLICES

CARROT CAKE

½ cup warm water

3 tablespoons ground flaxseeds

1¼ cups sorghum flour, plus more for sprinkling the pans

¾ cup teff flour

½ cup arrowroot starch

2½ teaspoons ground cinnamon

1¼ teaspoons xanthan gum

1¼ teaspoons baking soda

1 teaspoon baking powder

1 teaspoon fine sea salt

¼ teaspoon ground nutmeg

1½ cups unrefined cane sugar

¾ cup unsweetened applesauce

½ cup plus 1 tablespoon coconut oil, melted

1 teaspoon vanilla extract

1 cup raisins

1 tablespoon tapioca flour

4 cups grated carrots, grated with a box grater (see tip)

1 cup walnuts or pecans, toasted (see sidebar, page 13) and chopped (*omit for nut-free)

½ cup canned crushed pineapple, drained (reserve the juice for the filling)

To make the cake, preheat the oven to 350 degrees F. Lightly oil two 9-inch round baking pans. Sprinkle with sorghum flour, tapping out the excess.

Put the water in the bowl of a stand mixer, with the paddle attachment, or a large bowl. Stir in the flaxseeds and let stand until thickened, about 5 minutes.

Put the sorghum flour, teff flour, arrowroot starch, cinnamon, xanthan gum, baking soda, baking powder, salt, and nutmeg in a medium bowl. Stir with a dry whisk until combined.

Add the sugar, applesauce, coconut oil, and vanilla extract to the flaxseed mixture. Turn the stand mixer or a hand mixer on medium speed and beat until combined, about 2 minutes.

Turn the mixer to low speed. Gradually add the flour mixture, mixing until just combined. Turn off the mixer. Put the raisins in a small bowl. Add the tapioca flour and toss until the raisins are evenly coated. Add the carrots, raisin mixture, walnuts, and pineapple to the batter. Stir with a spoon until just mixed.

Scrape the batter into the prepared pans using a rubber spatula. Smooth the tops with the spatula. Bake in the center of the oven for 30 to 40 minutes, until a toothpick inserted in the center of each cake comes out clean. The cakes will be golden brown, begin to pull away from the sides of the pans, and will spring back when lightly touched.

Let cool in the pans for 10 minutes. Carefully remove the cakes from the pans and put them on a cooling rack. Let cool to room temperature while you prepare the filling and frosting.

To make the filling, put the pineapple juice and cornstarch in a small saucepan. (If you don't have enough pineapple juice, make up the difference with another juice or water.) Whisk until the cornstarch is dissolved. Stir in the agave nectar. Bring to a simmer over medium heat, stirring constantly. Do not boil. Decrease the heat to low and simmer

Per slice: 549 calories, 7 g protein, 25 g fat (16 g sat), 85 g carbs, 370 mg sodium, 80 mg calcium, 8 g fiber

PINEAPPLE FILLING

⅔ cup pineapple juice
(reserved from the drained
pineapple in the cake)

1½ tablespoons cornstarch

**1 tablespoon light agave
nectar, plus more as
needed**

½ teaspoon vanilla extract

⅛ teaspoon turmeric
(for color; optional)

COCONUT CREAM FROSTING

½ cup coconut butter
(preferably homemade;
see page 13)

1 teaspoon vanilla extract

**1½ cups confectioners'
sugar, sifted, plus more
as needed**

2 tablespoons coconut cream
(see page 14) **or full-fat
canned coconut milk, plus
more as needed**

until thickened, about 2 minutes. Immediately remove from the heat. Stir in the vanilla extract and optional turmeric. Scrape the filling into a small bowl using a rubber spatula. Let cool to room temperature, stirring often to prevent a skin from forming. Once the filling has cooled slightly, taste for sweetness. Stir in up to 1 tablespoon additional agave nectar, 1 teaspoon at a time, if desired.

To make the frosting, put the coconut butter and vanilla extract in the bowl of a stand mixer, with the paddle attachment, or a large bowl. Turn the mixer or a hand mixer to medium-high speed. Beat for 1 minute. Turn the mixer to low speed. Add the confectioners' sugar, ¼ cup at a time, until well mixed. Add the coconut cream. Turn the mixer to high speed and beat until fluffy, about 2 minutes. Add up to ½ cup additional confectioners' sugar, 2 tablespoons at a time, or 1 tablespoon additional coconut cream, 1 teaspoon at a time, until the frosting is thick, creamy, and spreadable.

To assemble the cake, carefully transfer one layer to a serving dish or cake stand. Spread the filling evenly over the top of the layer using a metal offset spatula. Cover with the other layer, pressing down lightly. Spread the frosting over the top and sides of the cake using the metal offset spatula. Serve immediately.

Stored in a sealed container, the cake will keep for 3 days at room temperature or 2 months in the freezer. Wrapped tightly in plastic wrap and stored in a sealed container, individual cake layers will keep for 3 days at room temperature or 2 months in the freezer.

TIP: Use a box grater, not a food processor, to grate the carrots. Carrots grated in a food processor release excess moisture, which will make the cake soggy.

When I asked family and friends to name their favorite cake, I wasn't surprised when the result was a tie between carrot cake and chocolate cake. Chocolate Carrot Cake is the **sweet marriage** of these top contenders. The silky chocolate frosting features wonderfully **wholesome ingredients.**

Chocolate Carrot Cake WITH GOOD-FOR-YOU FROSTING

FREE OF: LEGUMES, NUTS, PEANUTS, YEAST   YIELD: 12 SLICES

CHOCOLATE CARROT CAKE

¾ cup warm water

3 tablespoons ground flaxseeds

¾ cup sorghum flour

½ cup unsweetened cocoa powder, sifted, plus more for sprinkling the pans

½ cup quinoa flour or millet flour (see tip)

½ cup arrowroot starch

2 teaspoons baking soda

2 teaspoons ground cinnamon

1½ teaspoons xanthan gum

1 teaspoon baking powder

¾ teaspoon ground nutmeg

½ teaspoon fine sea salt

⅛ teaspoon ground cloves

3 cups grated carrots, grated with a box grater (see tip, page 43)

¾ cup light agave nectar

Scant ½ cup unsweetened applesauce

2 tablespoons canola oil

1 tablespoon vanilla extract

1 cup nondairy semisweet chocolate chips

To make the cake, preheat the oven to 350 degrees F. Lightly oil two 9-inch round cake pans. Sprinkle with cocoa powder, tapping out the excess.

Put ½ cup of the water in a large bowl. Stir in the flaxseeds and let stand until thickened, about 5 minutes.

Put the sorghum flour, cocoa powder, quinoa flour, arrowroot starch, baking soda, cinnamon, xanthan gum, baking powder, nutmeg, salt, and cloves in a medium bowl. Stir with a dry whisk until combined.

Add the carrots, agave nectar, applesauce, oil, and vanilla extract to the flaxseed mixture. Mix well. Add the flour mixture to the carrot mixture. Stir until just combined. Stir in the chocolate chips and the remaining ¼ cup of water until well incorporated.

Scrape the batter into the prepared pans using a rubber spatula. Smooth the tops with the spatula. Bake in the center of the oven for 25 to 30 minutes, until a toothpick inserted in the center of each cake comes out clean. The cakes will begin to pull away from the sides of the pans and will spring back when lightly touched.

Let cool in the pans for 10 minutes. Carefully remove the cakes from the pans and put them on a cooling rack. Let cool to room temperature before you prepare the frosting.

Per slice: 343 calories, 6 g protein, 13 g fat (5 g sat), 59 g carbs, 164 mg sodium, 73 mg calcium, 8 g fiber

GOOD-FOR-YOU FROSTING

½ cup pitted soft honey dates (see tip)

½ cup unsweetened cocoa powder, sifted

1 large ripe avocado, flesh removed

1 tablespoon light agave nectar

1 tablespoon vanilla extract

1 teaspoon ground cinnamon

Water, as needed

To make the frosting, put the dates, cocoa powder, avocado flesh, agave nectar, vanilla extract, and cinnamon in a food processor. Process until smooth. Add water, 1 teaspoon at a time, as needed to create a smooth, spreadable consistency.

To assemble the cake, carefully transfer one layer to a serving dish or cake stand. Spread the frosting evenly over the top using a metal offset spatula. Cover with the other layer, pressing down lightly. Generously spread the frosting over the top and sides of the cake. Serve at room temperature or refrigerate for up to 1 hour before serving.

Stored in a sealed container, the cake will keep for 3 days at room temperature or 2 months in the freezer. Wrapped tightly in plastic wrap and stored in a sealed container, individual cake layers will keep for 3 days at room temperature and 2 months in the freezer.

TIPS

- Millet flour and quinoa flour both work well in this recipe, but if you're keeping the cake for leftovers, I recommend using millet flour. The strong flavor of the quinoa flour will become more pronounced as the cake stands.

- If the dates are very firm, soak them in warm water for at least 20 minutes before making the frosting. For extra flavor and natural sweetness, use the soaking water when making the frosting.

VARIATION: For a more classic version, replace the Good-For-You Frosting with Chocolate Buttercream Frosting (page 39).

Similar to a classic blueberry buckle, this crumb cake is brimming with blueberries. Make Wild Blueberry Brunch Cake at the height of blueberry season. If possible, use wild blueberries in this cake, which is perfectly designed to showcase each juicy morsel.

Wild Blueberry BRUNCH CAKE

FREE OF: LEGUMES, NUTS, PEANUTS, SEEDS   YIELD: 9 PIECES

CINNAMON-SUGAR TOPPING

⅓ cup sorghum flour

⅓ cup unrefined cane sugar

½ teaspoon ground cinnamon

⅛ teaspoon fine sea salt

3 tablespoons coconut oil, softened
    (see page 18), **plus more as needed**

BLUEBERRY CAKE

1 cup sorghum flour

½ cup millet flour or quinoa flour
    (see tip, page 45)

½ cup tapioca flour

2 teaspoons baking powder

2 teaspoons finely grated lemon zest

1 teaspoon xanthan gum

½ teaspoon fine sea salt

¾ cup unrefined cane sugar

¼ cup coconut oil, softened or melted
    (see page 18)

¾ cup plus 2 tablespoons canned lite
    or full-fat coconut milk

2 teaspoons vanilla extract

2 teaspoons cider vinegar

2 cups fresh or frozen wild blueberries

To make the topping, put the sorghum flour, sugar, cinnamon, and salt in a small bowl. Add the coconut oil and stir until well combined. Stir in up to 1 tablespoon additional coconut oil, 1 teaspoon at a time, as needed to achieve a crumbly but not dry consistency.

To make the cake, preheat the oven to 375 degrees F. Lightly oil an 8-inch square glass baking dish.

Put the sorghum flour, millet flour, tapioca flour, baking powder, lemon zest, xanthan gum, and salt in a medium bowl. Stir with a dry whisk until combined.

Put the sugar and coconut oil in the bowl of a stand mixer, with the paddle attachment, or a large bowl. Using the stand mixer or a hand mixer, beat on medium speed until creamy and well combined. Add ¼ cup of the coconut milk, the vanilla extract, and vinegar. Beat until well combined.

Turn the mixer to low speed. Alternately add the flour mixture (in three additions) and the remaining coconut milk (in two additions), beginning and ending with the flour mixture, beating well after each addition. Turn off the mixer. Stir in the blueberries using a spoon. The batter will be very thick.

Scrape the batter into the prepared dish using a rubber spatula. Smooth the top with the spatula. Sprinkle evenly with the topping. Bake in the center of the oven for 40 to 55 minutes, until golden brown and a toothpick inserted in the center of the cake comes out clean. If using fresh blueberries, check the cake after it has baked for 40 minutes. Frozen and very juicy blueberries will require a longer baking time, 50 to 55 minutes. Let cool for at least 30 minutes before glazing.

Per piece: 362 calories, 3 g protein, 13 g fat (11 g sat), 61 g carbs, 219 mg sodium, 42 mg calcium, 4 g fiber

LEMON GLAZE

½ cup confectioners' sugar, sifted

2 teaspoons freshly squeezed lemon juice

¾ teaspoon vanilla extract

1 teaspoon nondairy milk or canned lite or full-fat coconut milk, plus more as needed

To make the glaze, about 10 minutes before serving, put the confectioners' sugar in a small bowl. Add the lemon juice and vanilla extract. Mix well. Stir in the nondairy milk until smooth, adding up to 1 teaspoon additional nondairy milk as needed to achieve a runny consistency. Spoon the glaze over the cake. Serve warm or at room temperature directly from the dish.

Stored in the baking dish and covered tightly with plastic wrap, the cake will keep for 3 days at room temperature. Stored in a sealed container, it will keep for 2 months in the freezer.

BAKERY

Cookies & Cakes

This simple cake, which features the **fruity flavor** of olive oil and a hint of citrus, is excellent for **brunch or tea.** The addition of cornmeal imparts an appealing texture.

ORANGE–OLIVE OIL Cake

FREE OF: LEGUMES, NUTS, PEANUTS, SEEDS   YIELD: 8 SLICES

½ cup sorghum flour, plus more for sprinkling the pan

½ cup arrowroot starch

½ cup stone-ground cornmeal

¾ cup millet flour or quinoa flour (see tip, page 45)

2 teaspoons baking powder

1 teaspoon xanthan gum

½ teaspoon fine sea salt

¾ teaspoon baking soda

2 teaspoons finely grated orange zest (about 1 medium orange)

¾ cup plus 2 tablespoons unrefined cane sugar

½ cup extra-virgin olive oil

½ cup unsweetened applesauce

½ cup freshly squeezed orange juice

½ teaspoon cider vinegar

Preheat the oven to 375 degrees F. Lightly oil a 9-inch round baking pan. Sprinkle with sorghum flour, tapping out the excess.

Put the sorghum flour, arrowroot starch, cornmeal, millet flour, baking powder, xanthan gum, salt, and baking soda in a medium bowl. Stir with a dry whisk until combined. Add the orange zest and stir with the whisk until evenly distributed.

Put ¾ cup of the sugar and the oil and applesauce in the bowl of a stand mixer, with the paddle attachment, or a large bowl. Turn the mixer or a hand mixer to medium speed. Beat until well combined. Add the orange juice and vinegar. Beat until well combined.

Turn the mixer to low speed. Add the flour mixture to the sugar mixture, beating until just mixed.

Scrape the batter into the prepared pan using a rubber spatula. Smooth the top with the spatula. Sprinkle with the remaining 2 tablespoons of sugar. Bake in the center of the oven for 25 to 30 minutes, until a toothpick inserted in the center of the cake comes out clean. The cake will be golden brown, begin to pull away from the sides of the pan, and will spring back when lightly touched.

Let cool in the pan for 10 minutes. Carefully remove the cake from the pan and put it on a cooling rack. Let cool for 20 minutes, then transfer to a serving dish. Serve warm or at room temperature.

Wrapped tightly in plastic wrap and stored in a sealed container, the cake will keep for 2 days at room temperature or 2 months in the freezer.

Glazed Orange–Olive Oil Cake: To dress up this cake, add a glaze. Put 6 tablespoons of confectioners' sugar, 2 to 3 teaspoons of freshly squeezed orange juice, and ¼ teaspoon of finely grated orange zest in a small bowl and mix until smooth. Drizzle over the cooled cake.

Per slice: 317 calories, 2 g protein, 15 g fat (2 g sat), 29 g carbs, 252 mg sodium, 44 mg calcium, 4 g fiber

True to its name, this **simple** cake comes together in minutes. When blackberries aren't in season, try substituting other seasonal fruits (see variation). Serve alongside **fresh iced tea** in the summertime or a steaming mug of apple cider come fall.

SIMPLE BLACKBERRY Buttermilk Cake

FREE OF: LEGUMES, NUTS, PEANUTS, SEEDS

YIELD: 8 SLICES

½ cup sorghum flour

¼ cup millet flour or quinoa flour (see tip, page 45)

¼ cup arrowroot starch

1 teaspoon baking powder

½ teaspoon baking soda

½ teaspoon xanthan gum

½ teaspoon finely grated lemon zest

¼ teaspoon fine sea salt

½ cup plus 1½ teaspoons unrefined cane sugar

3 tablespoons coconut oil, melted

½ teaspoon vanilla extract

¾ cup vegan buttermilk (see sidebar, page 17)

Scant 1 cup fresh blackberries, rinsed and dried

Confectioners' sugar, sifted, for dusting (optional)

Preheat the oven to 400 degrees F. Lightly oil a 9-inch round baking pan. Line the pan with parchment paper and lightly oil the parchment paper.

Put the sorghum flour, millet flour, arrowroot starch, baking powder, baking soda, xanthan gum, lemon zest, and salt in a medium bowl. Stir with a dry whisk until combined.

Put ½ cup of the sugar and the coconut oil and vanilla extract in the bowl of a stand mixer, with the paddle attachment, or a large bowl. Turn the mixer or a hand mixer to medium speed. Beat until well combined.

Turn the mixer to low speed. Alternately add the flour mixture (in three additions) and the vegan buttermilk (in two additions), beginning and ending with the flour mixture, beating well after each addition. Turn off the mixer.

Scrape the batter into the prepared pan using a rubber spatula. Smooth the top with the spatula. Scatter the blackberries over the batter. Sprinkle with the remaining 1½ teaspoons of sugar. Bake in the center of the oven for 20 to 25 minutes, until a toothpick inserted in the center of the cake comes out clean. The cake will be golden brown, begin to pull away from the sides of the pan, and will spring back when lightly touched.

Let cool in the pan for 10 minutes. Carefully remove the cake from the pan and put it on a cooling rack. Let cool for 20 minutes. Dust with confectioners' sugar if desired. Serve warm.

Wrapped tightly in plastic wrap and stored in a sealed container, the cake will keep for 2 days at room temperature or 2 months in the freezer.

Cranberry-Cinnamon Buttermilk Cake: Replace the blackberries with 1 cup of fresh or frozen cranberries. Sprinkle the top with ½ teaspoon of ground cinnamon in addition to the sugar before baking.

Per slice: 163 calories, 2 g protein, 6 g fat (5 g sat), 28 g carbs, 201 mg sodium, 67 mg calcium, 3 g fiber

A fresh take on the **beloved classic,** this two-layer dessert combines biscuit-style shortcake with fresh whipped cream, tangy lemon curd, and juicy strawberries.

NEW OLD-FASHIONED Strawberry Shortcake

FREE OF: LEGUMES, NUTS, PEANUTS, SEEDS   YIELD: 8 PORTIONS

STRAWBERRY FILLING AND TOPPING

4 cups sliced fresh strawberries

1½ tablespoons unrefined cane sugar (optional)

BISCUIT-STYLE SHORTCAKE

1 cup sorghum flour, plus more for sprinkling the pan

⅓ cup millet flour or quinoa flour (see tip, page 45)

⅓ cup arrowroot starch

⅓ cup cornstarch

¼ cup unrefined cane sugar

2 teaspoons baking powder

1 teaspoon xanthan gum

½ teaspoon baking soda

¼ teaspoon fine sea salt

1½ cups full-fat canned coconut milk

2 teaspoons cider vinegar

To make the filling and topping, put the strawberries and optional sugar in a large bowl. Refrigerate for 1 hour to soften.

To make the cake, preheat the oven to 400 degrees F. Lightly oil an 8-inch square baking pan. Sprinkle with sorghum flour, tapping out the excess.

Put the sorghum flour, millet flour, arrowroot starch, cornstarch, sugar, baking powder, xanthan gum, baking soda, and salt in a large bowl. Stir with a dry whisk until combined. Add the coconut milk and vinegar to the flour mixture. Mix until just combined.

Scrape the batter into the prepared pan using a rubber spatula. Smooth evenly. Bake in the center of the oven for 18 to 20 minutes, until a toothpick inserted in the center of the cake comes out clean.

Let cool in the pan for 5 minutes. Carefully remove the cake from the pan and put it on a cooling rack. Let cool while you prepare the lemon curd and whipped cream. (Alternatively, make the lemon curd while the shortcake is baking.)

To make the lemon curd, put the lemon zest, lemon juice, and cornstarch in a small saucepan. Whisk until the cornstarch is dissolved. Stir in the agave nectar and nondairy milk. Bring to a simmer over medium heat, stirring constantly. Do not boil. Decrease the heat to low and simmer until thickened, about 2 minutes. Remove from the heat. Stir in the vanilla extract and optional turmeric. Taste for sweetness, adding additional agave nectar if desired. Scrape the mixture into a small bowl using a rubber spatula. Let cool for 15 minutes at room temperature, then refrigerate until thickened, about 20 minutes. If the mixture becomes too thick, whisk briskly until smooth, adding 1 to 2 teaspoons of water as needed to achieve the consistency of thick jam.

Per portion: 493 calories, 5 g protein, 28 g fat (23 g sat), 57 g carbs, 226 mg sodium, 45 mg calcium, 5 g fiber

LEMON CURD

Finely grated zest of 2 lemons
(about 2 tablespoons)

6 tablespoons freshly squeezed
lemon juice

1½ tablespoons cornstarch

3 tablespoons light agave nectar,
plus more as needed

3 tablespoons nondairy milk

1 teaspoon vanilla extract

⅛ teaspoon turmeric (for color,
optional)

WHIPPED CREAM

2 (14-ounce) cans full-fat coconut milk,
refrigerated at least 24 hours

1 tablespoon confectioners' sugar,
sifted

1 teaspoon vanilla extract

To make the whipped cream, put a metal stand mixer bowl or large metal bowl and wire beaters in the freezer for at least 20 minutes before using. When you are ready to make the whipped cream, remove the bowl and beaters from the freezer and the coconut milk cans from the refrigerator. Do not shake the cans. Carefully open each can and spoon out the hardened coconut cream from the top of each can (save the coconut water that remains for drinking or using in a smoothie if desired). Put the coconut cream in the chilled metal bowl. Add the confectioners' sugar and vanilla extract. Using a stand mixer or hand mixer fitted with the chilled wire beaters, beat on high until creamy and fluffy. Refrigerate for 10 minutes.

To assemble the cake, remove the strawberries, lemon curd, and whipped cream from the refrigerator. Cut the cake in half laterally, using a sharp serrated knife, to make two layers. Carefully transfer the bottom layer to a serving dish or cake stand. Spread the lemon curd evenly over the top of the bottom layer using a metal offset spatula. Top with half of the whipped cream, followed by half of the strawberries. Carefully spread one-quarter to one-half of the remaining whipped cream over the strawberries and cover with the other cake layer. Top with the remaining whipped cream and strawberries.

The cake is best served when still slightly warm. It should be eaten the day it's made.

TIP: The coconut milk for the whipped cream must be refrigerated for at least 24 hours in advance, and a metal bowl and beaters must be chilled in the freezer for at least 20 minutes before using, so plan accordingly.

VARIATION: For a late-summer treat, replace the strawberries with 4 cups of peeled and sliced fresh peaches.

If you love apples, you'll love this cake, which features fresh apples and applesauce and is doused in a tangy apple cider sauce.

AUTUMN Apple Cake WITH CIDER SAUCE

FREE OF: LEGUMES,* NUTS, PEANUTS   YIELD: 15 PIECES

APPLE CAKE

½ cup apple cider

3 tablespoons ground flaxseeds

1¼ cups sorghum flour

1 cup millet flour

½ cup tapioca flour

¼ cup arrowroot starch

1 tablespoon ground cinnamon

1½ teaspoons xanthan gum

1½ teaspoons baking powder

1 teaspoon baking soda

1 teaspoon fine sea salt

1⅓ cups unrefined cane sugar

½ cup coconut oil, softened (see page 18)

¾ cup unsweetened applesauce

2 teaspoons vanilla extract

4 cups cored and cubed tart baking apples, such as Mutsu or Granny Smith (see tip)

To make the cake, preheat the oven to 325 degrees F. Oil a 13 x 9-inch glass baking dish.

Put the apple cider in a small microwave-safe bowl and microwave on high until warm, about 30 seconds. To warm on the stovetop, put the apple cider in a small saucepan and bring to a simmer over medium-high heat. Remove from the heat. Stir in the flaxseeds and let stand until thickened, about 5 minutes.

Put the sorghum flour, millet flour, tapioca flour, arrowroot starch, cinnamon, xanthán gum, baking powder, baking soda, and salt in a medium bowl. Stir with a dry whisk until combined.

Put the sugar and coconut oil in the bowl of a stand mixer, with the paddle attachment, or a large bowl. Using the stand mixer or a hand mixer, beat on medium-high speed until smooth and creamy, about 2 minutes. Turn the mixer to medium speed. Add the flaxseed mixture, applesauce, and vanilla extract. Beat until well combined, about 2 minutes.

Turn the mixer to low speed. Gradually add the flour mixture to the sugar mixture, beating until just combined. Turn off the mixer. Add the apples. Stir with a spoon just until evenly distributed. The batter will be thick.

Scrape the batter into the prepared dish using a rubber spatula. Smooth the top with the spatula. Bake in the center of the oven for 50 to 55 minutes, until a toothpick inserted in the center of the cake comes out clean. The cake will be golden brown. Let cool in the dish while you prepare the sauce.

Per piece: 283 calories, 3 g protein, 9 g fat (7 g sat), 52 g carbs, 272 mg sodium, 69 mg calcium, 4 g fiber

APPLE CIDER SAUCE

2 cups apple cider

1 tablespoon unrefined cane sugar,
   plus more as needed

⅓ cup nondairy milk

1 tablespoon arrowroot starch or
   cornstarch

1 teaspoon vegan buttery spread
   (optional; *omit for legume-free)

To make the sauce, put the apple cider in a small sauce-pan. Bring to a boil over high heat and boil until reduced to ¾ cup, about 15 minutes. Stir in the sugar until dissolved (for a sweeter sauce, use up to 1 tablespoon additional sugar as desired). While the cider is reducing, pour the nondairy milk into a small bowl. Add the arrowroot starch and whisk until the mixture is smooth. Pour the nondairy milk mixture into the apple cider reduction. Decrease the heat to low and let simmer until thickened, about 2 minutes, stirring once or twice. Remove from the heat. Stir in the optional vegan buttery spread. Let cool for 15 minutes.

About 10 minutes before serving, poke holes in the cake using a wooden skewer or toothpick. Pour the sauce over the cake. Serve warm or at room temperature. The flavor of this cake will improve if it sits for at least 30 minutes before serving.

Stored in the baking dish and covered tightly with plastic wrap, the cake will keep for 3 days at room temperature. Stored in a sealed container, it will keep for 2 months in the freezer.

TIP: Don't bother peeling the apples for this cake. You won't be able to detect the peel once the cake is baked.

In addition to being soaked in dark rum, conventional **holiday fruitcakes** are heavy on the butter and candied fruits. This version is reminiscent of the classic but omits the alcohol, added fat, and sugared fruit. Even people who shun conventional fruitcakes **will love it**.

Festive FRUIT AND NUT CAKE

FREE OF: LEGUMES, PEANUTS

YIELD: 16 SLICES

½ cup plus 2 tablespoons apple cider

3 tablespoons ground flaxseeds

⅔ cup unrefined cane sugar

¼ cup sorghum flour

¼ cup teff flour

¼ cup tapioca flour

2 teaspoons ground cinnamon

1 teaspoon ground cardamom

¾ teaspoon baking powder

¾ teaspoon ground nutmeg

½ teaspoon xanthan gum

½ teaspoon fine sea salt

¼ teaspoon baking soda

¼ teaspoon ground cloves

1½ cups pitted soft honey dates, chopped (see page 11)

¾ cup unsulfured dried apricots, cut in half

¾ cup unsulfured dried cherries

1 cup almonds, toasted (see sidebar, page 13)

1 cup pecans, toasted (see sidebar, page 13)

½ cup hazelnuts, toasted (see sidebar, page 13)

½ cup walnuts, toasted (see sidebar, page 13)

1½ teaspoons vanilla extract

Preheat the oven to 300 degrees F. Lightly oil an 8½ x 4½-inch loaf pan. Line with parchment paper and oil the parchment paper.

Put the apple cider in a small microwave-safe bowl and microwave on high until warm, about 30 seconds. To warm on the stovetop, put the apple cider in a small saucepan and bring to a simmer over medium-high heat. Remove from the heat. Stir in the flaxseeds and let stand until thickened, about 5 minutes.

Put the sugar, sorghum flour, teff flour, tapioca flour, cinnamon, cardamom, baking powder, nutmeg, xanthan gum, salt, baking soda, and cloves in a large bowl. Stir with a dry whisk until combined. Add the dates, apricots, cherries, almonds, pecans, hazelnuts, and walnuts and stir with a spoon until coated with the flour mixture.

Stir the vanilla extract into the flaxseed mixture. Pour the flaxseed mixture into the flour mixture. Mix until well combined.

Scrape the batter into the prepared pan using a rubber spatula, pressing it evenly into the pan with the spatula. Bake in the center of the oven for 55 to 60 minutes, until golden brown and a toothpick inserted in the center of the cake comes out clean. (Make sure to insert the toothpick in the cake, not the dried fruit). Tent with aluminum foil if the cake appears to be overbrowning.

Let cool completely in the pan, then carefully remove the cake from the pan. Though the cake can be eaten the day it's made, the flavor improves as it sits. I recommend wrapping the cake tightly in plastic wrap, then covering it with aluminum foil and waiting 5 days before eating. Stored this way, the cake will keep for 2 weeks at room temperature, 3 weeks in the refrigerator, or 3 months in the freezer. When serving, cut the cake using a sharp serrated or electric knife.

Per slice: 292 calories, 5 g protein, 15 g fat (1 g sat), 39 g carbs, 103 mg sodium, 80 mg calcium, 5 g fiber

This traditional Greek Lenten cake is moist, dense, and **not too sweet.** I prefer to replace the traditional sugar-syrup topping with a light sprinkling of confectioners' sugar to let the flavor of the tahini shine through. As a self-proclaimed "tahiniholic," I count this unique cake among my favorites.

GREEK Tahinopita

FREE OF: LEGUMES, NUTS,* PEANUTS, YEAST

YIELD: 10 SLICES

1 cup roasted tahini

¾ cup unrefined cane sugar

1 tablespoon finely grated orange zest (about 1 large orange)

1¼ cups sorghum flour, plus more for sprinkling the pan

½ cup quinoa flour

¼ cup arrowroot starch

¼ cup tapioca flour

2½ teaspoons baking powder

2 teaspoons xanthan gum

1 teaspoon ground cinnamon

½ teaspoon ground nutmeg

½ teaspoon ground allspice (optional)

½ teaspoon ground cloves (optional)

½ teaspoon baking soda

¼ teaspoon fine sea salt

1 cup freshly squeezed orange juice

¾ cup raisins

½ cup walnuts, chopped (optional; *omit for nut-free)

Confectioners' sugar, sifted, or agave nectar, for garnish

Preheat the oven to 350 degrees F. Lightly oil a 9-inch round baking pan. Sprinkle with sorghum flour, tapping out the excess.

Put the tahini, sugar, and orange zest in the bowl of a stand mixer, with the paddle attachment, or a large bowl. Turn the mixer or a hand mixer to medium-high speed. Beat until very creamy, about 7 minutes, occasionally stopping to scrape down the bowl with a rubber spatula if necessary.

Put the sorghum flour, quinoa flour, arrowroot starch, tapioca flour, baking powder, xanthan gum, cinnamon, nutmeg, optional allspice, optional cloves, baking soda, and salt in a medium bowl. Stir with a dry whisk until combined.

Turn the mixer to low speed. Alternately add the flour mixture (in three additions) and the orange juice (in two additions), beginning and ending with the flour mixture, beating well after each addition. Turn off the mixer. Stir in the raisins and optional walnuts. The mixture will be very stiff, similar to a thick cookie batter.

Scrape the batter into the prepared pan using a rubber spatula. If the batter is difficult to spread, dip the spatula into warm water. Bake in the center of the oven for 30 to 35 minutes, until a toothpick inserted in the center of the cake comes out clean. The cake will be golden brown and begin to pull away from the sides of the pan.

Let cool in the pan for 5 minutes. Carefully remove the cake from the pan and put it on a cooling rack. Sprinkle with confectioners' sugar or generously brush with agave nectar before serving.

Wrapped tightly in plastic wrap and stored in a sealed container at room temperature, the cake will keep for 2 days.

Per slice: 399 calories, 8 g protein, 15 g fat (2 g sat), 66 g carbs, 257 mg sodium, 85 mg calcium, 5 g fiber

Anything but ordinary, this traditional Armenian cake is **moist and fluffy** inside, providing a unique contrast to its sugary crisp crust. You'll love the **unexpected combination** of textures, not to mention the **spicy kick** of nutmeg.

Armenian NUTMEG CAKE

FREE OF: NUTS,* PEANUTS   YIELD: 10 SLICES

3 tablespoons warm water

1 tablespoon ground flaxseeds

1 cup sorghum flour, plus more for sprinkling the pan

½ cup plus 2 tablespoons teff flour

½ cup plus 2 tablespoons arrowroot starch or tapioca flour

2 teaspoons baking powder

1½ teaspoons xanthan gum

¼ teaspoon fine sea salt

1½ cups unrefined cane sugar

½ cup vegan buttery spread, softened

1 cup nondairy milk

1 teaspoon baking soda

2 teaspoons ground nutmeg

½ teaspoon cider vinegar

½ cup walnuts or pecans, chopped (*omit for nut-free)

Preheat the oven to 350 degrees F. Lightly oil a 9-inch round baking pan or springform pan. Sprinkle with sorghum flour, tapping out the excess.

Put the water in a small bowl or measuring cup. Stir in the flaxseeds and let stand until thickened, about 5 minutes.

Put the sorghum flour, ½ cup of the teff flour, ½ cup of the arrowroot starch, and the baking powder, xanthan gum, and salt in a large bowl. Stir with a dry whisk until combined. Add the sugar and mix well with the whisk. Rub the vegan buttery spread into the flour mixture using your fingers, until the mixture resembles coarse crumbs.

Scoop 2¼ loosely packed cups of the flour mixture into the prepared pan. Use your fingers to firmly press the mixture over the bottom and about ¾ inch up the sides of the pan.

Put the nondairy milk in a small bowl. Stir in the baking soda until dissolved. Add the flaxseed mixture and nutmeg. Mix well. Stir in the vinegar. Working quickly, pour the nondairy milk mixture into the remaining flour mixture. Mix well. Add the remaining 2 tablespoons of teff flour and 2 tablespoons of arrowroot starch. Mix until just combined.

Scrape the batter into the pan using a rubber spatula and spread it evenly. Sprinkle with the walnuts. Bake in the center of the oven for 45 to 55 minutes, until a toothpick inserted in the center of the cake comes out clean.

Let cool completely in the pan. Serve directly from the pan or transfer to a serving dish.

Stored in a sealed container, the cake will keep for 2 days at room temperature or 2 months in the freezer.

Per slice: 339 calories, 4 g protein, 14 g fat (3 g sat), 55 g carbs, 340 mg sodium, 104 mg calcium, 4 g fiber

Cupcakes & Mini Cakes

And above all, watch with glittering eyes the whole world around you because the greatest secrets are always hidden in the most unlikely places.

ROALD DAHL, *THE MINPINS*

See Strawberry-Vanilla Glazed Cupcakes, page 66.

upcakes and mini cakes are special. It might be because they're already in perfect, individual portions. Or perhaps it's because a generous schmear of sweetness tops each one. Or maybe it's because cupcakes are hidden by whimsical wrappers, and you can only reveal the bliss within by peeling away the paper and taking a bite. Whatever the reason, these single-serve cakes call out to us—and we love them for it.

TIPS FOR PERFECTING THE CUPCAKE

Equipment

- Line a 12-cup standard muffin pan with paper liners or coat the cups with vegan buttery spread or oil. I recommend liners for mess-free cleanup, serving, and storage.

- When using a 24-cup mini muffin pan, coat the cups with oil instead of using liners for quick and easy two-bite snacking.

- To prevent paper liners from sticking to the cupcakes, spritz them lightly with oil before filling. Gluten-free cupcake batter can be sticky, especially when fruit is used.

- Fill each cup of a standard muffin pan about two-thirds full. If you overfill the cups, you risk having sunken or overflowing cupcakes.

Baking

- Bake cupcakes in the center of the oven. If there are two or more pans, leave at least one inch of space between the pans and the sides of the oven for proper heat circulation.

- Don't open the oven door until it's time to check the cupcakes for doneness. The cool air will affect the rising.

- To check for doneness, insert a toothpick in the center of a cupcake. If there is filling inside, insert the toothpick slightly to the side. It should come out clean and free of crumbs. Alternatively, lightly press the top of a cupcake with your fingers. If the indentation springs back, the cupcake is done.

- When the cupcakes are finished baking, let them cool in the pan for about 5 minutes, then transfer them to a wire rack to cool completely.

Troubleshooting

Since cupcakes are simply small cakes, the same troubleshooting techniques apply. If your cupcakes don't turn out perfect the first time, see table 7 (page 26) for helpful modifications.

TIPS FOR MAKING MINI CAKES

hen I need an individual dessert that is slightly more sophisticated and a bit larger than a cupcake, I bake miniature-sized cakes in ramekins. The result is a sweet and classy treat worthy of any dinner party. Any basic cupcake batter recipe can be used to create mini cakes. (See Individual Pear-Cardamom Upside-Down Cakes, page 79, and Molten Lava Mini Cakes with Raspberry Sauce, page 76, for specific recipes.)

- Use four-inch ramekins for mini cakes. Oil them and fill each one about two-thirds full to give the batter room to rise.
- Bake the mini cakes at the same temperature given in the cupcake recipe.
- Bake for 22 to 25 minutes. In general, mini cakes need to bake a couple of minutes longer than cupcakes.
- To check for doneness, insert a toothpick in the center of the mini cake. If it comes out clean, free of crumbs, the mini cake is done.
- When mini cakes are finished baking, let them cool in the ramekins for about 5 minutes, then run a knife around the edge of each cake to loosen it from the sides of the ramekin. Turn each one out onto an individual serving dish.
- Mini cakes are best served warm; if there are leftovers, reheat before serving.
- For an elegant presentation, top each mini cake with a scoop of nondairy ice cream, a handful of fresh berries, and a dusting of confectioners' sugar.

FROSTING TECHNIQUES

- When frosting cupcakes, stay basic by using a metal offset spatula (see page 26) or butter knife. For fancier effects, use a cake-decorating bag or tool.
- If using a metal offset spatula or butter knife, scoop a generous schmear of frosting onto the top of the cupcake. Hold the cupcake in one hand and the spatula or knife in the other for controlled spreading.

- If using a cake-decorating bag or tool, fit it with the desired tip (a star tip is among the most common). Start by piping the frosting around the outer edge of the cupcake. Continue to pipe, working inward to create a coil until you reach the center of the cupcake. Pull up the tip with a twist of your wrist to get a nice finished swirl.
- See Cakes (page 28) for additional frosting techniques.
- Cupcakes and mini cakes can be mixed and matched with various frostings, glazes, and other toppings for the ultimate flavor combination. For inspiration, see Mixing and Matching Cakes and Frostings, page 29.

PANIFICIO · PASTICCERIA

Cashew fans, prepare for a double dose in these moist cupcakes, which feature **rich and creamy** cashew butter in the cake *and* the buttercream frosting. The frosting is also luscious sandwiched between a couple of **fresh-baked** cookies. Or, if desired, try it on other cupcakes or cakes.

Cashew Butter CUPCAKES

FREE OF: PEANUTS, SEEDS

YIELD: 10 LARGE CUPCAKES

CASHEW BUTTER CUPCAKES

½ cup creamy roasted cashew butter (see tip)

3 tablespoons canola oil or coconut oil, melted

½ cup light agave nectar

6 tablespoons unsweetened applesauce

2 teaspoons vanilla extract

1 teaspoon cider vinegar

¾ cup sorghum flour

½ cup arrowroot starch

¼ cup quinoa flour

2 teaspoons baking powder

1 teaspoon xanthan gum

½ teaspoon fine sea salt

6 tablespoons nondairy milk, plus more as needed

To make the cupcakes, preheat the oven to 350 degrees F. Line a 12-cup standard muffin pan with 10 paper liners.

Put the cashew butter and oil in the bowl of a stand mixer, with the paddle attachment, or a large bowl. Turn the mixer or a hand mixer to medium speed. Beat until smooth and creamy, about 3 minutes. Add the agave nectar. Beat until well combined. Add the applesauce, vanilla extract, and vinegar. Beat until smooth and well mixed.

Put the sorghum flour, arrowroot starch, quinoa flour, baking powder, xanthan gum, and salt in a medium bowl. Stir with a dry whisk until combined.

Turn the mixer to low speed. Alternately add the flour mixture (in three additions) and the nondairy milk (in two additions), beginning and ending with the flour mixture, beating well after each addition. Turn off the mixer. The batter will be thick but should be spreadable (see tip).

Spoon the batter into the pan, evenly filling each of the 10 cups about two-thirds full. Smooth the tops with moistened fingertips if desired. Bake in the center of the oven for 15 to 20 minutes, until a toothpick inserted in the center of a cupcake comes out clean and the top of the cupcake springs back when lightly touched.

Let cool in the pan for 10 minutes. Carefully remove the cupcakes from the pan and put them on a cooling rack to cool completely before you prepare the frosting.

Per cupcake: 382 calories, 5 g protein, 19 g fat (3 g sat), 51 g carbs, 206 mg sodium, 64 mg calcium, 2 g fiber

CASHEW BUTTER BUTTERCREAM FROSTING

- **6 tablespoons creamy roasted cashew butter** (see tip)
- **3 tablespoons vegan buttery spread**
- **2 teaspoons vanilla extract**
- **1¼ cups confectioners' sugar, sifted, plus more as needed**
- **1 tablespoon nondairy milk, plus more as needed**
- **Chopped cashews, cacao nibs, or nondairy semisweet chocolate chips** (optional)

To make the frosting, put the cashew butter, vegan buttery spread, and vanilla extract in the bowl of a stand mixer, with the paddle attachment, or a large bowl. Beat until creamy, about 2 minutes. Add ¾ cup of the confectioners' sugar. Beat until smooth and creamy, about 2 minutes longer. Add the remaining ½ cup of confectioners' sugar and the nondairy milk. Turn the mixer to high speed and beat until light and fluffy, 3 to 5 minutes, adding up to 1 tablespoon additional nondairy milk, 1 teaspoon at a time, as needed until a spreadable consistency is achieved. Generously top each cupcake with the frosting. Garnish with the optional cashews, cacao nibs, or chocolate chips.

Serve immediately or keep at room temperature until serving time. The cashew flavor will become more pronounced as the cupcakes stand.

Stored in a sealed container, the cupcakes will keep for 3 days at room temperature or 2 months in the freezer.

TIP: Because different brands of cashew butter will vary in consistency, you may need to adjust the amounts of other ingredients in the cupcake batter and frosting. The batter should be very thick but spreadable; if it isn't spreadable, add 1 to 3 tablespoons additional nondairy milk, 1 tablespoon at a time, until a spreadable consistency is achieved. If the frosting is too thin, you may need to add more confectioners' sugar.

This is the **quintessential** chocolate cupcake recipe. These cupcakes are **light and moist,** and they have just the right amount of chocolate flavor.

Chocolate Cupcakes WITH CHOCOLATE FROSTING

FREE OF: LEGUMES, NUTS, PEANUTS, SEEDS   YIELD: 12 CUPCAKES

CHOCOLATE CUPCAKES

¾ cup unrefined cane sugar

½ cup sorghum flour

6 tablespoons teff flour

6 tablespoons arrowroot starch

⅓ cup unsweetened cocoa powder, sifted

1½ teaspoons xanthan gum

¾ teaspoon baking soda

½ teaspoon baking powder

½ teaspoon fine sea salt

½ teaspoon ground cinnamon

1 cup brewed coffee (see tip, page 39)

⅓ cup coconut oil, melted

1 teaspoon vanilla extract

1 teaspoon cider vinegar

CHOCOLATE FROSTING

3 tablespoons coconut oil, softened (see page 18)

1 teaspoon vanilla extract

3½ cups confectioners' sugar, sifted

½ cup unsweetened cocoa powder, sifted

1 tablespoon nondairy milk, plus more as needed

Per cupcake: 334 calories, 2 g protein, 11 g fat (10 g sat), 61 g carbs, 184 mg sodium, 22 mg calcium, 3 g fiber

To make the cupcakes, preheat the oven to 350 degrees F. Line a 12-cup standard muffin pan with 12 paper liners.

Put the sugar, sorghum flour, teff flour, arrowroot starch, cocoa powder, xanthan gum, baking soda, baking powder, salt, and cinnamon in a medium bowl. Stir with a dry whisk until combined.

Put the coffee, coconut oil, vanilla extract, and vinegar in a medium bowl. Mix briskly, until smooth and well combined, about 2 minutes.

Make a well in the center of the flour mixture. Pour the coffee mixture into the well and stir until well combined using a rubber spatula.

Spoon the batter into the pan, filling each of the 12 cups about two-thirds full. Bake in the center of the oven for 15 to 20 minutes, until a toothpick inserted in the center of a cupcake comes out clean and the top of the cupcake springs back when lightly touched.

Let cool in the pan for 10 minutes. Carefully remove the cupcakes from the pan and put them on a cooling rack to cool completely before you prepare the frosting.

To make the frosting, put the coconut oil and vanilla extract in the bowl of a stand mixer, with the paddle attachment, or a large bowl. Using the stand mixer or a hand mixer, beat until creamy and smooth, about 3 minutes. Add the confectioners' sugar and cocoa powder, continuing to beat until well mixed. Add the nondairy milk, 1 teaspoon at a time, and mix just until a smooth, thick consistency is achieved. If the frosting is too dry, add up to 1 more tablespoon of nondairy milk, 1 teaspoon at a time, until the frosting is thick but spreadable. Generously top each cupcake with the frosting.

Stored in a sealed container, the cupcakes will keep for 2 days at room temperature or 2 months in the freezer.

Chocolate Cupcakes with Chocolate-Macadamia Frosting: Prepare the cupcakes as directed. Instead of the Chocolate Frosting, make the Peanut Butter Buttercream Frosting (page 35) using macadamia nut butter instead of peanut butter. Mix in ¼ cup of sifted unsweetened cocoa powder before adding the confectioners' sugar.

Sweet pineapple and tangy orange are loving companions in these moist, tender cupcakes.

ORANGE-PINEAPPLE Cupcakes

FREE OF: LEGUMES, PEANUTS, NUTS, SEEDS   YIELD: 10 CUPCAKES

ORANGE-PINEAPPLE CUPCAKES

⅓ cup millet flour

⅓ cup sorghum flour

⅓ cup arrowroot starch

1 tablespoon cornstarch

1 tablespoon finely grated orange zest (about 1 large orange)

1 teaspoon xanthan gum

¾ teaspoon baking powder

¼ teaspoon baking soda

¼ teaspoon fine sea salt

½ cup canned pineapple tidbits, drained

½ cup nondairy milk

¼ cup coconut oil, melted

½ cup unrefined cane sugar

1 teaspoon cider vinegar

1 teaspoon vanilla extract

ORANGE GLAZE

¾ cup confectioners' sugar, sifted

½ teaspoon finely grated orange zest

1 tablespoon freshly squeezed orange juice, plus more as needed

To make the cupcakes, preheat the oven to 350 degrees F. Line a 12-cup standard muffin pan with 10 paper liners.

Put the millet flour, sorghum flour, arrowroot starch, cornstarch, orange zest, xanthan gum, baking powder, baking soda, and salt in a large bowl. Stir with a dry whisk until combined.

Put the pineapple, nondairy milk, and coconut oil in a food processor or blender. Process until smooth. Add the sugar, vinegar, and vanilla extract. Process again until smooth and well combined.

Make a well in the center of the flour mixture. Scrape the pineapple mixture into the well using a rubber spatula. Mix until combined using the spatula.

Spoon the batter into the pan, evenly filling each of the 10 cups about two-thirds full. Bake in the center of the oven for 23 to 25 minutes, until a toothpick inserted in the center of a cupcake comes out clean and the top of the cupcake springs back when lightly touched.

Let cool in the pan for 10 minutes. Carefully remove the cupcakes from the pan and put them on a cooling rack to cool completely before you prepare the glaze.

To make the glaze, put the confectioners' sugar in a small bowl. Add the orange zest and orange juice. Mix until smooth. If the glaze is too thick, add up to 1 tablespoon additional orange juice, 1 teaspoon at a time, until the desired consistency is achieved. Dip the top of each cupcake in the glaze, letting any excess drip off. Let stand until the glaze has set, about 15 minutes.

Stored in a sealed container, the cupcakes will keep for 3 days at room temperature or 2 months in the freezer.

Per cupcake: 179 calories, 1 g protein, 6 g fat (5 g sat), 32 g carbs, 116 mg sodium, 37 mg calcium, 2 g fiber

Each one of these light vanilla cupcakes comes with a **sweet surprise** tucked inside.

Strawberry-Vanilla GLAZED CUPCAKES

FREE OF: LEGUMES, NUTS,* PEANUTS, SEEDS   YIELD: 12 CUPCAKES

STRAWBERRY-VANILLA CUPCAKES

½ cup sorghum flour

⅓ cup arrowroot starch

¼ cup millet flour

¼ cup quinoa flour

1¼ teaspoons baking powder

1 teaspoon xanthan gum

¼ teaspoon baking soda

¼ teaspoon fine sea salt

⅔ cup light agave nectar

⅔ cup nondairy milk

⅓ cup coconut oil, melted

2 teaspoons vanilla extract

2 teaspoons cider vinegar

12 small fresh strawberries,
    washed, dried, and hulled
    (see tip)

To make the cupcakes, preheat the oven to 325 degrees F. Line a 12-cup standard muffin pan with 12 paper liners.

Put the sorghum flour, arrowroot starch, millet flour, quinoa flour, baking powder, xanthan gum, baking soda, and salt in a large bowl. Stir with a dry whisk until combined.

Put the agave nectar, nondairy milk, coconut oil, vanilla extract, and vinegar in a small bowl. Mix well. Pour the agave nectar mixture into the flour mixture. Stir until well combined.

Spoon the cupcake batter into the pan, evenly filling each of the 12 cups about two-thirds full. Press a whole strawberry, tip-side down, into the center of each one, pushing down lightly so the strawberry is just submerged. If necessary, use the spoon to cover the top of the strawberry with batter. Bake in the center of the oven for 20 to 25 minutes, until a toothpick inserted in the center of a cupcake (not the strawberry) comes out clean.

Let cool in the pan for 10 minutes. Carefully remove the cupcakes from the pan and put them on a cooling rack to cool completely before you prepare the glaze.

Per cupcake: 206 calories, 1 g protein, 7 g fat (6 g sat), 36 g carbs, 114 mg sodium, 47 mg calcium, 2 g fiber

VANILLA GLAZE

2 tablespoons nondairy milk

1 teaspoon vanilla extract

½ teaspoon almond extract
(*omit for nut-free)

1 cup confectioners' sugar, sifted

To make the glaze, pour the nondairy milk into a medium microwave-safe bowl. Microwave on high until warm, about 30 seconds. Alternatively, pour the nondairy milk into a small saucepan. Bring to a simmer over medium-high heat until warm, about 3 minutes. Remove from the heat. Stir in the vanilla extract and almond extract. Gradually add the confectioners' sugar, about ¼ cup at a time, stirring until well mixed and smooth. Dip the top of each cupcake in the glaze, letting any excess drip off. Let stand until the glaze has set, about 15 minutes. Serve at room temperature.

Stored in a sealed container, the cupcakes will keep for 2 days at room temperature or 2 months in the freezer.

TIP: To achieve the best balance of cake to fruit, choose fresh, locally grown strawberries that are no more than 1½ inches tall or wide. Be sure the strawberries are thoroughly dry before using.

Strawberry-Vanilla Cupcakes with Bakery-Style White Frosting:
Prepare the cupcakes as directed. Instead of the glaze, make Thick Vanilla Frosting (page 75), omitting the lemon juice and adding ¼ teaspoon of almond extract. Generously top each cupcake with the frosting.

These **chai-spiced** cupcakes call for banana in both the batter and the creamy frosting. The result is a **sweet-and-spicy** treat. If you're a true chai aficionado, feel free to add a little more spice (see tip).

Banana-Chai CUPCAKES

FREE OF: NUTS, PEANUTS, SEEDS   YIELD: 10 CUPCAKES

BANANA-CHAI CUPCAKES

½ cup sorghum flour

½ cup millet flour or quinoa flour
(see tip, page 45)

¼ cup arrowroot starch

1 tablespoon cornstarch

2 teaspoons ground cinnamon

2 teaspoons ground cardamom

1 teaspoon ground ginger

1 teaspoon xanthan gum

1 teaspoon baking powder

¼ teaspoon baking soda

¼ teaspoon ground cloves

¼ teaspoon ground nutmeg

¾ cup unrefined cane sugar

½ cup mashed very ripe banana

⅓ cup coconut oil, melted

2 teaspoons vanilla extract

⅔ cup vegan buttermilk (see
sidebar, page 17)

To make the cupcakes, preheat the oven to 350 degrees F. Line a 12-cup standard muffin pan with 10 paper liners.

Put the sorghum flour, millet flour, arrowroot starch, cornstarch, cinnamon, cardamom, ginger, xanthan gum, baking powder, baking soda, cloves, and nutmeg in a large bowl. Stir with a dry whisk until combined.

Put the sugar, banana, coconut oil, and vanilla extract in the bowl of a stand mixer, with the paddle attachment, or a large bowl. Turn the stand mixer or a hand mixer to medium speed. Beat until smooth and creamy, about 2 minutes.

Turn the mixer to low speed. Alternately add the flour mixture (in three additions) and the vegan buttermilk (in two additions), beginning and ending with the flour mixture, beating well after each addition. Turn off the mixer. The batter will be thick.

Spoon the batter into the pan, evenly filling each of the 10 cups about two-thirds full. Smooth the tops with moistened fingertips if desired. Bake in the center of the oven for 18 to 22 minutes, until a toothpick inserted in the center of a cupcake comes out clean and the top of the cupcake springs back when lightly touched.

Let cool in the pan for 10 minutes. Carefully remove the cupcakes from the pan and put them on a cooling rack to cool completely before you prepare the frosting.

Per cupcake: 393 calories, 2 g protein, 13 g fat (8 g sat), 71 g carbs, 113 mg sodium, 54 mg calcium, 3 g fiber

BANANA FROSTING

1 small ripe banana, well mashed

½ teaspoon freshly squeezed lemon juice

¼ cup vegan buttery spread

3 cups confectioners' sugar, sifted, plus more as needed

GARNISH

12 slices ripe banana, about ⅛ inch thick

Ground cinnamon

To make the frosting, put the banana and lemon juice in the bowl of a stand mixer, with the paddle attachment, or a large bowl. Turn the stand mixer or hand mixer to medium speed. Beat until well combined, about 30 seconds. Add the vegan buttery spread. Beat until well mixed, about 2 minutes. Add the confectioners' sugar, about ½ cup at a time, and continue beating until the frosting is thick but spreadable. If the frosting is too thin, add more confectioners' sugar, 1 tablespoon at a time, until the desired consistency is achieved. Generously top each cupcake with the frosting. Garnish each cupcake with 1 banana slice and a sprinkle of cinnamon.

Stored in a sealed container, the cupcakes will keep for 3 days at room temperature or 2 months in the freezer.

TIP: While I like the balance of spices in this recipe, you can alter the amounts to please your own palate. If you aren't familiar with cardamom, for example, try using half of the specified amount. If you love a strong chai flavor, you may want to double the spices.

French toast is at its best when made from **cinnamon bread** and doused in pure maple syrup. French Toast Cupcakes, which have a **cinnamon-sugar swirl** and delicious maple glaze, take their cue from this breakfast favorite.

French Toast CUPCAKES

FREE OF: NUTS, PEANUTS, SEEDS   YIELD: 10 CUPCAKES

CINNAMON-SUGAR SWIRL

2 tablespoons unrefined cane sugar

1 1/2 teaspoons ground cinnamon

1 teaspoon unsweetened cocoa powder

MAPLE CUPCAKES

1/2 cup millet flour

1/2 cup sorghum flour

1/4 cup tapioca flour

1 teaspoon baking powder

3/4 teaspoon xanthan gum

1/4 teaspoon baking soda

1/4 teaspoon fine sea salt

2 tablespoons vegan buttery spread

2 tablespoons coconut oil, softened (see page 18)

1/4 cup unrefined cane sugar

6 tablespoons pure maple syrup (preferably grade B)

1 teaspoon vanilla extract

1/2 cup plus 1 tablespoon vegan buttermilk (see sidebar, page 17)

1 1/2 teaspoons cider vinegar

To make the swirl, put the sugar, cinnamon, and cocoa powder in a small bowl. Mix well.

To make the cupcakes, preheat the oven to 350 degrees F. Line a 12-cup standard muffin pan with 10 paper liners.

Put the millet flour, sorghum flour, tapioca flour, baking powder, xanthan gum, baking soda, and salt in a large bowl. Stir with a dry whisk until combined.

Put the vegan buttery spread and coconut oil in the bowl of a stand mixer, with the paddle attachment, or a large bowl. Turn the stand mixer or a hand mixer to medium speed. Beat until well combined, about 30 seconds. Add the sugar. Beat until creamy and fluffy, about 2 minutes. Add the maple syrup and vanilla extract. Beat until well mixed.

Turn the mixer to low speed. Alternately add the flour mixture (in three additions) and the vegan buttermilk (in two additions), beginning and ending with the flour mixture, beating well after each addition. Turn off the mixer. Add the vinegar and briskly stir with a rubber spatula until just combined.

Spoon a heaping tablespoon of the batter into each of the 10 cups. Evenly distribute the cinnamon-sugar mixture on top of the batter. Divide the remaining batter evenly among the cups until they are about two-thirds full. Bake in the center of the oven for 20 to 25 minutes, until a toothpick inserted in the center of a cupcake comes out clean and the top of the cupcake springs back when lightly touched.

Let cool in the pan for 10 minutes. Carefully remove the cupcakes from the pan and put them on a cooling rack to cool completely before you prepare the glaze.

Per cupcake: 221 calories, 2 g protein, 6 g fat (3 g sat), 43 g carbs, 148 mg sodium, 55 mg calcium, 2 g fiber

MAPLE SYRUP GLAZE

- **1 cup confectioners' sugar, sifted**
- **2 tablespoons pure maple syrup** (preferably grade B)
- **½ teaspoon maple extract**
- **1 teaspoon nondairy milk, plus more as needed**

To make the glaze, put the confectioners' sugar in a small bowl. Add the maple syrup and maple extract. Mix until smooth. Add the nondairy milk and mix well, adding up to 1 teaspoon additional nondairy milk, a little at a time, as needed to achieve a smooth, thick consistency; the glaze should not be runny. Dip the top of each cupcake in the glaze, letting any excess drip off. Let stand until the glaze has set, about 15 minutes.

Stored in a sealed container, the cupcakes will keep for 2 days at room temperature or 2 months in the freezer.

VARIATION: To top these cupcakes with frosting instead of the glaze, use Maple Buttercream Frosting (page 105).

Have a sweet tooth? These **tempting** cupcakes are guaranteed to satisfy. Serve warm, topped with Whipped Cream (page 51) or a scoop of nondairy **ice cream,** alongside a cup of dark-roasted coffee.

Sticky Date Cupcakes WITH TOFFEE CHOCOLATE SAUCE

FREE OF: NUTS, PEANUTS, SEEDS, YEAST

YIELD: 10 CUPCAKES

STICKY DATE CUPCAKES

1 ¼ cups pitted soft honey dates
  (see page 11)

1 cup water

1 teaspoon baking soda

½ cup sorghum flour

¼ cup tapioca flour

¼ cup teff flour

1 teaspoon baking powder

½ teaspoon xanthan gum

¼ teaspoon ground ginger

⅛ teaspoon fine sea salt

⅔ cup unrefined cane sugar

3 tablespoons vegan buttery spread

¼ cup unsweetened applesauce

2 tablespoons nondairy milk

1 teaspoon vanilla extract

To make the cupcakes, preheat the oven to 350 degrees F. Lightly oil 10 cups of a 12-cup standard muffin pan. Don't use paper liners for this recipe.

Put the dates and water in a medium saucepan. The water should cover the dates. Bring to a boil over high heat and cook for 3 minutes. Remove from the heat. Stir in the baking soda. The mixture may smell bad—don't worry, this is normal. Let stand for 10 minutes. Mash the mixture to a paste using a fork.

Put the sorghum flour, tapioca flour, teff flour, baking powder, xanthan gum, ginger, and salt in a medium bowl. Stir with a dry whisk until combined.

Put the sugar and vegan buttery spread in the bowl of a stand mixer, with the paddle attachment, or a large bowl. Turn the stand mixer or a hand mixer to medium speed. Beat until smooth and creamy, about 2 minutes. Add the applesauce, nondairy milk, and vanilla extract. Beat until well combined.

Turn the mixer to low speed. Add the flour mixture. Beat until well mixed. Turn off the mixer. Stir in the date mixture using a rubber spatula, being careful not to fully incorporate it; some swirls should remain.

Spoon the batter into the pan, evenly filling each of the 10 cups about two-thirds full. Bake in the center of the oven for 18 to 22 minutes, until a toothpick inserted in the center of a cupcake comes out clean and the top of the cupcake springs back when lightly touched. Prepare the sauce while the cupcakes are baking.

Per cupcake: 286 calories, 2 g protein, 7 g fat (2 g sat), 57 g carbs, 229 mg sodium, 46 mg calcium, 3 g fiber

TOFFEE CHOCOLATE SAUCE

1 cup light agave nectar

½ cup lite or full-fat canned coconut milk

2 tablespoons vegan buttery spread

⅛ teaspoon fine sea salt

2 tablespoons nondairy semisweet chocolate chips

To make the sauce, put the agave nectar, coconut milk, vegan buttery spread, and salt in a medium saucepan. (The mixture will bubble very high, so be sure to use a larger saucepan than you think you might need.) Cook over medium-high heat until reduced and thick enough to coat the back of a spoon, 12 to 20 minutes. Add the chocolate chips and stir until the chocolate has melted and the mixture is smooth, about 30 seconds. Immediately remove from the heat. Pour the sauce into a large measuring cup or small bowl and let cool for 10 minutes.

When the cupcakes are finished baking, keep the oven at 350 degrees F. Remove the cupcakes from the oven and let cool in the pan for 5 minutes. Carefully flip each cupcake onto its side and let cool in the pan for 10 minutes longer.

Transfer the cupcakes to a 9-inch square baking dish, allowing a bit of room around each of the cupcakes so they can be removed easily when serving. Pour the sauce over the cupcakes. Bake for 5 minutes.

Stored in the baking dish and covered tightly with plastic wrap, the cupcakes will keep for 3 days in the refrigerator. The sauce will harden when chilled, so microwave the cupcakes until warm, 20 to 30 seconds, or warm them in the oven at 300 degrees F for 8 to 10 minutes before serving.

TIP: If desired, Sticky Date Cupcakes with Toffee Chocolate Sauce can be made in two stages. Prepare and bake the cupcakes as directed. Let cool and store in a sealed container at room temperature. When ready to serve, preheat the oven to 350 degrees F. Prepare the Toffee Chocolate Sauce and put the cupcakes in the baking dish as directed. Pour the sauce over the cupcakes and bake for 5 minutes.

If you love chocolate-covered cherries, you'll become a fan of these mini cupcakes. Stuffed with cherries and topped with a thick vanilla frosting coated in chocolate, these cupcakes impress with both their tempting appearance and great taste.

TWO-BITE Chocolate-Covered Cherry CUPCAKES

FREE OF: NUTS, PEANUTS, SEEDS, YEAST   YIELD: 24 MINI CUPCAKES

CHOCOLATE-CHERRY MINI CUPCAKES

½ cup unsweetened cocoa powder, sifted

½ cup teff flour

¼ cup sorghum flour

¼ cup tapioca flour

¾ teaspoon xanthan gum

½ teaspoon baking powder

½ teaspoon fine sea salt

¾ cup unrefined cane sugar

6 tablespoons unsweetened applesauce

6 tablespoons coconut oil, softened or melted (see page 18)

¼ cup nondairy milk

2 teaspoons vanilla extract

24 frozen pitted black or sour cherries, defrosted

To make the cupcakes, preheat the oven to 350 degrees F. Lightly oil a 24-cup mini muffin pan.

Put the cocoa powder, teff flour, sorghum flour, tapioca flour, xanthan gum, baking powder, and salt in a medium bowl. Stir with a dry whisk until combined.

Put the sugar, applesauce, coconut oil, nondairy milk, and vanilla extract in the bowl of a stand mixer, with the paddle attachment, or a large bowl. Using the stand mixer or the hand mixer, beat until smooth and well combined. The mixture might look curdled—don't worry, this is normal. Add the flour mixture. Beat until well mixed, occasionally stopping to scrape down the bowl with a rubber spatula if necessary.

Spoon 1 heaping tablespoon of the batter into each of the 24 mini muffin cups. Press a cherry into each cup, submerging each one halfway in the batter. Bake in the center of the oven for 12 to 18 minutes, until the edges are firm to the touch and a toothpick inserted in a cupcake comes out clean. Don't overbake. Let cool in the pan for about 10 minutes. Carefully remove the cupcakes from the pan and put them on a cooling rack to cool completely before frosting.

To make the frosting, put the vegan buttery spread and coconut oil in the bowl of a stand mixer, with the paddle attachment, or a large bowl. Using the stand mixer or the hand mixer, beat on medium-high speed until smooth and well combined. Add the vanilla extract, lemon juice, and 1 cup of the confectioners' sugar. Beat until smooth and creamy, about 2 minutes. Turn the mixer to low speed. Add the remaining confectioners' sugar, about ½ cup at a time, and continue beating until thick. Add the nondairy milk. Turn to high speed and beat until fluffy, about 5 minutes. The frosting should be very thick and creamy. If the frosting is too thin, add more confectioners' sugar, 1 tablespoon at a time, until the desired consistency is achieved.

Per cupcake: 237 calories, 2 g protein, 12 g fat (8 g sat), 34 g carbs, 75 mg sodium, 29 mg calcium, 2 g fiber

THICK VANILLA FROSTING

5 tablespoons vegan buttery spread

3 tablespoons coconut oil, softened (see page 18)

2½ teaspoons vanilla extract

1 teaspoon freshly squeezed lemon juice

3 cups confectioners' sugar, sifted, plus more as needed

2 teaspoons nondairy milk

CHOCOLATE COATING

1 cup nondairy semisweet chocolate chips

4 teaspoons canola oil

Transfer the frosting to a cake-decorating bag fitted with a ½-inch round pastry tip. Pipe a spiral of frosting, about 1½ inches high, on top of each cupcake. The frosting should be about the same height as the cupcake itself. Put the cupcakes on a plate or large cutting board. Put in the freezer for about 8 minutes, until the frosting is hard. While the cupcakes are in the freezer, make the chocolate coating.

To make the chocolate coating, put the chocolate chips and oil in a small microwave-safe bowl. Microwave on high for 15 seconds and stir. Repeat as needed until the chocolate has melted and the mixture is smooth. To melt the chocolate on the stovetop, fill a small saucepan with one inch of water. Bring to a simmer over medium heat. Put a glass bowl on top of the saucepan, making sure it doesn't touch the water but creates a seal to trap the steam produced by the simmering water. Put the chocolate chips and oil in the bowl. As the bowl heats, the chocolate will begin to melt. Stir occasionally, until the chocolate is completely melted. Scrape the chocolate coating into a small, deep container using a rubber spatula. The container should be deep enough so you can dip the frosting into it without scraping the container bottom. I use a ½-cup measuring cup, refilling it once.

Remove the cupcakes from the freezer. Pick up a cupcake, holding it by the bottom, and dip the frosting into the chocolate coating. Completely cover the frosting with the chocolate coating, letting any excess drip off. (If any frosting remains exposed, spoon some of the chocolate coating onto the exposed area.) Put the cupcake back on the plate. Repeat with the remaining cupcakes. Refrigerate for about 25 minutes before serving to let the chocolate coating set.

Stored in a sealed container in the refrigerator, the cupcakes will keep for 2 days.

TIP: If desired, the cupcakes can be baked one day before they are frosted and coated. Stored in a sealed container at room temperature, unfrosted, uncoated cupcakes will keep for 4 days. When ready to serve, prepare the frosting and chocolate coating as directed.

The secret behind this cake's chocolaty lava center is chocolate truffles, which are prepared in advance then tucked into the batter before baking. The molten center is spectacular in the larger cakes—which are perfect for sharing—and slightly more subtle in the smaller version (see the variation).

Molten Lava Mini Cakes WITH RASPBERRY SAUCE

FREE OF: LEGUMES, NUTS, PEANUTS, SEEDS

YIELD: 3 MINI CAKES

TRUFFLES FOR THE MOLTEN CENTER
(must be prepared at least 9 hours in advance)

- 1 cup nondairy semisweet chocolate chips
- ¼ cup full-fat canned coconut milk or coconut cream (page 14)

CHOCOLATE CAKE

- ½ cup sorghum flour
- ¼ cup teff flour
- ¼ cup arrowroot starch
- 6 tablespoons unrefined cane sugar
- 3 tablespoons unsweetened cocoa powder
- Scant ¾ teaspoon baking soda
- ½ teaspoon xanthan gum
- ¼ teaspoon fine sea salt
- 6 tablespoons nondairy milk
- ¼ cup coconut oil, melted
- 2 teaspoons cider vinegar
- 1 teaspoon vanilla extract

To make the truffles for the molten center, put the chocolate chips and coconut milk in a microwave-safe bowl. Microwave on high for 15 seconds and stir. Repeat as needed until the chocolate has melted and the mixture is smooth. To melt the chocolate on the stovetop, fill a small saucepan with one inch of water. Bring to a simmer over medium heat. Put a glass bowl on top of the saucepan, making sure it doesn't touch the water but creates a seal to trap the steam produced by the simmering water. Put the chocolate chips and coconut milk in the bowl. As the bowl heats, the chocolate will begin to melt. Stir occasionally, until the chocolate is completely melted, then transfer to a small bowl. Refrigerate until firm, about 3 hours.

Remove the chocolate mixture from the refrigerator. Scoop out 1 tablespoon of the mixture and roll it between your hands (this may get a little messy) to form a round truffle, about 1½ inches in diameter. Repeat to form 8 truffles in total. Put the truffles on a sheet of waxed paper in a container. Put the container in the freezer for at least 6 hours, until the truffles have set. (You won't need all the truffles for this recipe; leftovers can be stored in a sealed container in the freezer for up to 3 months.)

To make the mini cakes, preheat the oven to 400 degrees F. Generously oil three 6-ounce ramekins and put them on a baking sheet.

Put the sorghum flour, teff flour, arrowroot starch, sugar, cocoa powder, baking soda, xanthan gum, and salt in a medium bowl. Stir with a dry whisk until combined. Put the nondairy milk, coconut oil, vinegar, and vanilla extract in a small bowl. Mix well. Make a well in the center of the flour mixture. Pour the nondairy milk mixture into the well and stir until well combined using a rubber spatula.

Per mini cake: 611 calories, 8 g protein, 30 g fat (24 g sat), 85 g carbs, 522 mg sodium, 117 mg calcium, 11 g fiber

RASPBERRY SAUCE

1 cup fresh or frozen raspberries or frozen mixed berries (see tip)

6 tablespoons freshly squeezed orange juice

2 tablespoons water

2 teaspoons arrowroot starch

GARNISH

¼ cup confectioners' sugar, sifted, for dusting (optional)

Coconut cream (page 14), for drizzling (optional)

Spoon the batter into the prepared ramekins, evenly filling each about two-thirds full. Press a truffle into the center of each one, pushing down lightly so the truffle is covered with the batter. If necessary, use the spoon to cover the top of the truffle with batter. Bake in the center of the oven for 13 to 16 minutes, until a toothpick inserted near the edge of a cake comes out clean (don't insert the toothpick into the molten center). Do not overbake.

Let cool for 5 minutes directly in the ramekins. Make the sauce while the mini cakes are baking.

To make the sauce, put the raspberries and orange juice in a small saucepan. Cook over medium heat until the raspberries begin to break down, about 3 minutes. Put the water and arrowroot starch in a small bowl. Mix until smooth. Pour the arrowroot mixture into the raspberry mixture and mix well. Decrease the heat to medium-low and simmer until thickened, about 1 minute. Remove from the heat.

To assemble, run a knife around the edge of each mini cake to loosen it from the sides of the ramekins. Turn each mini cake out onto an individual serving dish. Drizzle each mini cake with one-third of the raspberry sauce. Dust with confectioners' sugar and drizzle with coconut cream if desired. Serve warm.

TIP: For a completely smooth sauce, strain the raspberry mixture through a fine wire sieve to remove the raspberry seeds before adding the arrowroot mixture. Return it to the saucepan and thicken as directed.

VARIATION: To make smaller portions, use four 4-ounce ramekins. Make the truffles slightly smaller, about 1¼ inch in diameter. Prepare the cakes as directed and bake for 11 to 13 minutes. Note that while the molten centers in the smaller cakes will still ooze, they won't ooze quite as much as the larger cakes.

Coconut lovers, this one is for you. Mini Triple-Coconut Cupcakes are loaded with coconut ingredients, then topped with a toasted coconut glaze.

MINI Triple-Coconut CUPCAKES

FREE OF: LEGUMES, NUTS, PEANUTS, SEEDS

YIELD: 24 MINI CUPCAKES

COCONUT MINI CUPCAKES

Scant 1 cup unrefined cane sugar

1/2 cup millet flour

1/2 cup sorghum flour

1/4 cup tapioca flour

1/4 cup arrowroot starch

1/3 cup unsweetened finely shredded dried coconut

1 teaspoon baking soda

3/4 teaspoon xanthan gum

1/2 teaspoon fine sea salt

1 cup lite or full-fat canned coconut milk

1/3 cup coconut oil, softened or melted (see page 18)

2 teaspoons vanilla extract

1 teaspoon cider vinegar

TOASTED COCONUT GLAZE

1 cup confectioners' sugar, sifted

1/4 cup lite or full-fat canned coconut milk, plus more as needed

3/4 cup unsweetened finely shredded dried coconut, toasted (see page 13)

To make the cupcakes, preheat the oven to 350 degrees F. Lightly oil a 24-cup mini muffin pan.

Put the sugar, millet flour, sorghum flour, tapioca flour, arrowroot starch, coconut, baking soda, xanthan gum, and salt in a large bowl. Stir with a dry whisk until combined.

Put the coconut milk, coconut oil, and vanilla extract in a medium bowl or large measuring cup. Stir with a whisk until well combined.

Make a well in the center of the flour mixture. Pour the coconut milk mixture into the well and stir until well combined using a rubber spatula. Add the vinegar and briskly stir with the rubber spatula until just combined.

Spoon the batter into the prepared pan, filling each of the 24 mini muffin cups about two-thirds full. Bake in the center of the oven for 15 to 20 minutes, until a toothpick inserted in the center of a cupcake comes out clean.

Let cool in the pan for 10 minutes. Carefully remove the cupcakes from the pan and put them on a cooling rack to cool completely before you prepare the glaze.

To make the glaze, put the confectioners' sugar in a small bowl. Add the coconut milk, 1 tablespoon at a time, mixing well after each addition. Use just enough coconut milk to obtain a smooth, thick consistency. If the glaze is too thick, add up to 1 tablespoon additional coconut milk, 1 teaspoon at a time. The glaze should not be runny.

Put the toasted coconut on a small plate. Dip the tops of the cupcakes in the glaze, letting any excess drip off, then into the toasted coconut. Let stand for 10 minutes before serving.

Stored in a sealed container, the cupcakes will keep for 3 days at room temperature or 2 months in the freezer.

Per cupcake: 136 calories, 1 g protein, 6 g fat (5 g sat), 19 g carbs, 100 mg sodium, 21 mg calcium, 1 g fiber

These little cakes are simple to prepare and call for relatively few ingredients, making them a great option for an **after-school snack** or postdinner treat. For an elegant dinner-party dessert, **serve warm** with a scoop of vanilla nondairy ice cream and a sprinkle of additional cardamom.

INDIVIDUAL PEAR-CARDAMOM Upside-Down Cakes

FREE OF: NUTS, PEANUTS, SEEDS   YIELD: 4 MINI CAKES

PEAR-CARDAMOM LAYER

4 teaspoons vegan buttery spread, softened

6 teaspoons unrefined cane sugar

1 large, ripe, firm pear, such as Bartlett, peeled and very thinly sliced (about ¼ inch thick)

¼ teaspoon ground cardamom (see tip)

BUTTERMILK CAKES

Scant ½ cup sorghum flour

2 tablespoons tapioca flour

1 teaspoon baking powder

¼ teaspoon xanthan gum

⅛ teaspoon baking soda

⅛ teaspoon fine sea salt

¼ cup unrefined cane sugar

6 tablespoons vegan buttermilk (see sidebar, page 17)

1 tablespoon vegan buttery spread, melted

½ teaspoon vanilla extract

To make the pear layer, divide the vegan buttery spread among four 6-ounce ramekins, coating the bottom of each ramekin. Sprinkle 1½ teaspoons of the sugar in each ramekin. Divide the pear equally among the ramekins, slightly overlapping the slices. Sprinkle the cardamom over the pears.

To make the mini cakes, preheat the oven to 350 degrees F. Put the sorghum flour, tapioca flour, baking powder, xanthan gum, baking soda, and salt in a medium bowl. Stir with a dry whisk until combined.

Put the sugar, vegan buttermilk, vegan buttery spread, and vanilla extract in a large measuring cup. Mix well. Pour the sugar mixture into the flour mixture. Mix until just combined. The mixture will be very fluffy.

Spoon the batter evenly over the pears in each ramekin, filling each about two-thirds full. Put the ramekins on a baking sheet. Bake for 20 to 25 minutes, until a toothpick inserted in the center of a cake comes out clean.

Let cool for 5 minutes directly in the ramekins. Run a knife around the edge of each mini cake to loosen it from the sides of the ramekins. Turn each mini cake out onto an individual serving dish so the pears are on top. Serve warm.

Stored in a sealed container in the refrigerator, the mini cakes will keep for 2 days; however, they are best served the day they are made.

TIP: If you love cardamom, add ⅛ to ¼ teaspoon additional cardamom for a spicier kick. If you're new to this flavor, stick to the specified amount.

Per mini cake: 229 calories, 2 g protein, 7 g fat (2 g sat), 42 g carbs, 258 mg sodium, 88 mg calcium, 3 g fiber

Cookies

And I had but one penny in the world, thou should'st have it to buy gingerbread.

WILLIAM SHAKESPEARE, *LOVE'S LABOR'S LOST*
See Traditional Gingerbread Men, page 106.

ere's something that everyone seems to agree on: cookies are fabulous. Who doesn't love a handheld treat that satisfies in just a few bites? Whether you crave a humble peanut butter cookie or a creamy sandwich cookie, you'll find it (and many others) in this chapter.

TIPS FOR CONQUERING THE COOKIE

Equipment

- To prevent cookies from sticking to the baking sheet and ensure easy cleanup, line the baking sheet with parchment paper or a reusable silicone baking mat.

- Some ovens can accommodate only one baking sheet at a time. In that case, just bake one batch of cookies at a time. Have a second baking sheet ready and waiting to put in immediately after the first batch is finished.

- If you don't have a cooling rack, put cookies on a sheet of waxed paper sprinkled with sugar to cool. This will prevent the cookies from becoming soggy.

Handling the Dough

- When cookie dough needs to be cut out or rolled out, refrigerate the dough beforehand, according to the recipe directions. Refrigeration makes the dough firmer and easier to handle, and it also helps to prevent the dough from spreading while baking. After removing the cookie dough from the refrigerator, let it sit at room temperature for five minutes before rolling.

- Before refrigerating cookie dough that will be rolled out, split the dough into two or more portions for easier rolling.

- Minimize rerolling leftover scraps of dough, as rerolling will cause the dough to become tough.

- When putting the cookie dough on the baking sheet, allow some room for spreading. Try arranging the cookies in staggered rows for proper heat circulation, which will also let you fit more on the sheet.

Baking

- Make cookies all the same size so they will finish baking at the same time.

- Try a small test batch before baking all the cookies, especially if you're in an unfamiliar climate, using new ingredients, or using new baking sheets.

If the test cookies spread too much, refrigerate the dough for about thirty minutes before trying again. If they don't spread at all, flatten the next batch with your palm before baking.

- Check for doneness at the minimum baking time given. Cookies are done when they are slightly firm to the touch and golden brown around the edges.

- When making drop cookies, alter the baking time to get the texture you prefer. For chewy or soft cookies, bake for one to two minutes less than the recipe specifies. For crispy cookies, bake for one to two additional minutes.

- When baking multiple batches, always use a baking sheet that is at room temperature or cool. If the baking sheet is still hot after being used for a previous batch, rinse it with tepid water to cool it down. Don't rinse with cold water or the baking sheet will warp.

Storage

- Most cookies are at their prime the day they are baked or the day after. The texture of some cookies will change considerably in just a few hours or even after one day. Follow the storage recommendations in each recipe for the best results. Also see table 8 for how to remedy leftover cookies that become stale or too soft.

TABLE 8 Troubleshooting when baking cookies

PROBLEM	POSSIBLE CAUSES AND SOLUTIONS
The cookies are too tough.	• The dough contained too much flour. • A new or substituted flour created different results. • The dough contained too little sugar or fat.
The cookies are crumbly.	• The dough contained too much sugar, fat, or leavening. • The dough wasn't mixed well.
The cookies are too dry.	• The dough contained too much flour or too little liquid. • The cookies were overbaked.
The cookies don't brown or are doughy.	• The oven temperature was set too low. • The cookies were underbaked. • Consider using baking sheets that don't have sides; the sides prevent the heat from circulating around the cookies.
The cookies spread too much.	• The dough contained too much sugar or fat or too little flour. • The vegan buttery spread or coconut oil was too soft. • The baking sheets were coated with too much oil (line the baking sheets with parchment paper instead). • Refrigerate the dough for 30 minutes before baking to prevent spreading.
The cookies were supposed to spread but did not.	• The dough contained too little sugar or fat. • The oven temperature was set too high.
The cookies are dark or burned.	• Dark pans (which are often nonstick) absorb more heat and transfer it to the cookies (see page 140 for pan recommendations). If using dark pans, decrease the oven temperature by 25 degrees F or decrease the baking time.
Leftover cookies became stale.	• Steam the cookies by putting them on a rack over a saucepan of simmering water until softened, about 1 minute.
Leftover cookies became too soft.	• Bake the cookies in a preheated oven at 300 degrees F for about 5 minutes.

Here is a welcome departure from the basic chocolate cookie. These soft cookies contain a sweet surprise—a creamy filling made of almond butter and chocolate chips.

CHOCOLATE-ALMOND BUTTER Surprises

FREE OF: PEANUTS, SEEDS, YEAST   YIELD: 12 COOKIES

CHOCOLATE COOKIES

½ cup unrefined cane sugar

¼ cup vegan buttery spread

1 tablespoon nondairy milk

½ teaspoon vanilla extract

½ cup sorghum flour

¼ cup tapioca flour or arrowroot starch

¼ cup unsweetened cocoa powder, sifted

1 teaspoon xanthan gum

½ teaspoon baking powder

⅛ teaspoon baking soda

⅛ teaspoon fine sea salt

To make the cookie dough, put the sugar and vegan buttery spread in the bowl of a stand mixer, with the paddle attachment, or a large bowl. Using the stand mixer or a hand mixer, beat on medium-high speed until fluffy, about 2 minutes. Add the non-dairy milk and vanilla extract. Beat until well combined.

Put the sorghum flour, tapioca flour, cocoa powder, xanthan gum, baking powder, baking soda, and salt in a medium bowl. Stir with a dry whisk until combined. Turn the mixer to low speed. Gradually add the flour mixture to the sugar mixture, beating until a soft dough forms. Turn off the mixer.

Put a large piece of plastic wrap on a flat surface. Scrape the dough onto the plastic wrap using a rubber spatula and form it into a ball. Wrap the dough tightly in the plastic wrap. Refrigerate for 30 minutes.

To make the filling, put the almond butter, confectioners' sugar, and chocolate chips in a small bowl. Mix with a spoon until well combined. The consistency should be similar to cookie dough. If the filling is too thin, add additional confectioners' sugar, 1 teaspoon at a time, until the desired consistency is achieved. If the filling is too thick, add additional almond butter, 1 teaspoon at a time, until the desired consistency is achieved.

To make the cookies, preheat the oven to 350 degrees F. Line a baking sheet with parchment paper or a silicone baking mat.

Remove the dough from the refrigerator. For each cookie, scoop 1 rounded tablespoon of dough into your hand. Roll into a ball between the palms of your hands. Flatten into a thin disk between your palms and put the disk on a flat surface. Put 1 teaspoon of the filling in the center of the disk and fold the sides of the dough around the filling. Flatten with your

Per cookie: 153 calories, 2 g protein, 8 g fat (2 g sat), 20 g carbs, 82 mg sodium, 29 mg calcium, 2 g fiber

CHOCOLATE–ALMOND BUTTER FILLING

5 tablespoons creamy roasted almond butter, plus more as needed

3 tablespoons confectioners' sugar, sifted, plus more as needed

1 tablespoon nondairy semisweet chocolate chips

palm. Put the cookie seam-side down on the lined baking sheet. Repeat with the remaining dough and filling.

Bake for 10 to 12 minutes, until the cookies are slightly firm to the touch. Let cool on the baking sheet for 5 minutes. Carefully remove the cookies from the baking sheet and put them on a cooling rack to cool completely.

Stored in a sealed container, the cookies will keep for 3 days at room temperature or 3 months in the freezer.

These **kid-friendly cookies** are light, airy, and refreshingly minty, making them a welcome alternative to the overly sweet fudge and iced treats that typically adorn the holiday cookie tray. This recipe also provides a solution for using up decorative **candy canes.**

HOLIDAY Candy Cane SNOWBALLS

FREE OF: NUTS, PEANUTS, SEEDS, YEAST   YIELD: 18 SNOWBALLS

½ cup vegan buttery spread

¾ cup confectioners' sugar, sifted

½ teaspoon vanilla extract

¼ teaspoon peppermint extract

¾ cup sorghum flour

¼ cup quinoa flour

¼ cup arrowroot starch

½ teaspoon xanthan gum

⅛ teaspoon fine sea salt

¼ cup finely crushed candy canes* (see tip)

*See pages 144 to 145 for suppliers of dye-free, organic candy canes.

Per snowball: 91 calories, 1 g protein, 5 g fat (1 g sat), 10 g carbs, 45 mg sodium, 1 mg calcium, 1 g fiber

Preheat the oven to 400 degrees F. Line a baking sheet with parchment paper or a silicone baking mat.

Put ¼ cup of the confectioners' sugar and the vegan buttery spread, vanilla extract, and peppermint extract in the bowl of a stand mixer, with the paddle attachment, or a large bowl. Using the stand mixer or a hand mixer, beat on medium-high speed until creamy and smooth, about 2 minutes.

Put the sorghum flour, quinoa flour, arrowroot starch, xanthan gum, and salt in a medium bowl. Stir with a dry whisk until combined. Turn the mixer to low speed. Gradually add the flour mixture to the sugar mixture, beating until a soft dough forms. Turn off the mixer and stir in the candy canes until well incorporated.

For each cookie, scoop out 1 rounded tablespoon of dough and roll it into a ball between the palms of your hands. Put the ball on the lined baking sheet. Repeat with the remaining dough.

Bake for 13 to 16 minutes, until the cookies are firm to the touch and starting to turn slightly golden around the edges. Don't overbake. Let cool on the baking sheet for 10 minutes, until all of the candy cane pieces have hardened. Carefully remove the cookies from the baking sheet and put them on a cooling rack to cool completely before coating.

Put the remaining ½ cup of confectioners' sugar in a small bowl. Carefully put a cookie in the bowl and coat generously with the confectioners' sugar, tapping off any excess. Return the cookie to the cooling rack. Repeat with the remaining cookies.

Stored in a sealed container, the cookies will keep for 4 days at room temperature or 3 months in the freezer.

TIPS

- To crush the candy canes, put them in a large ziplock bag. Seal the bag and roll over it with a rolling pin until the candy is crushed into fine pieces. For a therapeutic variation, ditch the rolling pin and use the bottom of a heavy mug—just take care not to damage the countertops.

- Use parchment paper or a silicone baking mat for this recipe. Because the candy canes ooze when baking, they will stick to an unlined baking sheet, making cleanup difficult.

Also known as Mexican wedding cakes, Russian tea cakes, Italian butter nuts, and snowballs, these popular cookies are commonly served during holidays and celebrations. However, don't wait for a special occasion to serve them; these sugarcoated shortbread cookies are a hit any time of the year.

Mexican WEDDING COOKIES

FREE OF: PEANUTS, SEEDS, YEAST   YIELD: 30 COOKIES

1¼ cups sorghum flour

½ cup arrowroot starch

¼ cup quinoa flour

1 teaspoon xanthan gum

¼ teaspoon fine sea salt

1 cup pecans, toasted
  (see sidebar, page 13),
  cooled, and finely ground

1 cup vegan buttery spread

1 cup confectioners' sugar,
  sifted

2 teaspoons vanilla extract

Preheat the oven to 325 degrees F. Line two baking sheets with parchment paper or silicone baking mats.

Put the sorghum flour, arrowroot starch, quinoa flour, xanthan gum, and salt in a large bowl. Stir with a dry whisk until combined. Stir in the pecans until evenly distributed.

Put the vegan buttery spread in the bowl of a stand mixer, with the paddle attachment, or a large bowl. Using the stand mixer or a hand mixer, beat on medium-high speed until fluffy, about 2 minutes. Add ½ cup of the confectioners' sugar and the vanilla extract. Beat until smooth.

Turn the mixer to low speed. Gradually add the flour mixture to the sugar mixture, beating until just combined. Turn off the mixer. Refrigerate the dough directly in the bowl for 15 minutes.

For each cookie, scoop out 1 rounded tablespoon of dough and roll it into a ball between the palms of your hands. Put the ball on a lined baking sheet. Repeat with the remaining dough.

Bake for 14 to 18 minutes, until the cookies are firm and slightly golden around the edges. Let cool on the baking sheets for 5 minutes. Carefully remove the cookies from the baking sheets and put them on a cooling rack for an additional 10 minutes.

Put the remaining ½ cup of confectioners' sugar in a small bowl. While the cookies are still warm, carefully put a cookie in the bowl and coat generously with the confectioners' sugar, tapping off any excess. Return the cookie to the cooling rack. Repeat with the remaining cookies. Let cool to room temperature before serving.

Stored in a sealed container, the cookies will keep for 4 days at room temperature or 3 months in the freezer.

Per cookie: 120 calories, 1 g protein, 9 g fat (2 g sat), 10 g carbs, 72 mg sodium, 3 mg calcium, 1 g fiber

These cookies feature the pleasant taste of tahini, a savory sesame paste. Don't worry—the sweetness of the maple syrup and chocolate balance out the tahini nicely, and this unique combination is just likely to make these cookies your new favorite.

CHOCOLATE CHUNK-TAHINI Cookies

FREE OF: LEGUMES, NUTS, PEANUTS, YEAST   YIELD: 20 LARGE COOKIES

½ cup plus 2 tablespoons sorghum flour

¼ cup quinoa flour

4 tablespoons tapioca flour, plus more as needed

½ teaspoon baking soda

½ teaspoon xanthan gum

½ teaspoon fine sea salt

¾ cup roasted tahini

¾ cup pure maple syrup (grade A or B)

1 teaspoon vanilla extract

1 cup nondairy chocolate chunks

Preheat the oven to 375 degrees F. Line a baking sheet with parchment paper or a silicone baking mat.

Put the sorghum flour, quinoa flour, tapioca flour, baking soda, xanthan gum, and salt in a medium bowl. Stir with a dry whisk until combined.

Put the tahini, maple syrup, and vanilla extract in the bowl of a stand mixer, with the paddle attachment, or a large bowl. Using the stand mixer or a hand mixer, beat on medium-high speed until well combined, about 2 minutes.

Turn the mixer to low speed. Gradually add the flour mixture to the tahini mixture, beating until just combined. The mixture should be sticky and stiff. If the mixture is runny, add up to 2 tablespoons additional tapioca flour, 1 teaspoon at a time, until a stiff consistency is achieved. Turn off the mixer. Stir in the chocolate chunks until evenly distributed.

For each cookie, scoop out 2 rounded tablespoons of dough and drop it onto the lined baking sheet. Use damp fingers to press the dough until it's about ½ inch thick. Repeat with the remaining dough, leaving about 2 inches between cookies for spreading.

Bake for 11 to 14 minutes, until the edges are just starting to turn golden (for chewy cookies) or until the edges are a little darker (for crunchy cookies). Even though the cookies may not look like they're done, do not overbake them. Let cool on the baking sheet for 5 minutes. Carefully remove the cookies from the baking sheet and put them on a cooling rack. Let cool to room temperature before serving.

Stored in a sealed container, the cookies will keep for 4 days at room temperature or 3 months in the freezer.

Per cookie: 177 calories, 3 g protein, 9 g fat (3 g sat), 23 g carbs, 117 mg sodium, 29 mg calcium, 2 g fiber

Everyone says their chocolate chip cookies are the best. Well, these really are. They're chewy on the inside, crispy on the edges, and big—just the way chocolate chip cookies should be.

Essential CHOCOLATE CHIP COOKIES

FREE OF: NUTS, PEANUTS, YEAST   YIELD: 16 LARGE COOKIES

¾ cup vegan buttery spread

2 tablespoons ground flaxseeds

1 cup plus 2 tablespoons
  sorghum flour

½ cup teff flour

½ cup tapioca flour

1 teaspoon xanthan gum

¾ teaspoon baking soda

½ teaspoon fine sea salt

1⅓ cups unrefined cane sugar

¼ cup nondairy milk

2 teaspoons vanilla extract

1 heaping cup nondairy
  semisweet chocolate chips

Preheat the oven to 325 degrees F. Line three baking sheets with parchment paper or silicone baking mats.

Put the vegan buttery spread in a medium saucepan. Warm over medium heat until just melted. Immediately remove from the heat. Stir in the flaxseeds and let stand until thickened, about 5 minutes.

Put the sorghum flour, teff flour, tapioca flour, xanthan gum, baking soda, and salt in a medium bowl. Stir with a dry whisk until combined.

Put the flaxseed mixture, sugar, nondairy milk, and vanilla extract in the bowl of a stand mixer, with the paddle attachment, or large bowl. Using the stand mixer or a hand mixer, beat on medium-high speed until well combined, about 2 minutes.

Turn the mixer to low speed. Gradually add the flour mixture to the sugar mixture, beating until just combined. Turn off the mixer. Stir in the chocolate chips until evenly distributed.

For each cookie, scoop out 3 rounded tablespoons of dough and drop it onto a lined baking sheet. Repeat with the remaining dough, leaving at least 4 inches between cookies for spreading. (Because the cookies are large, put no more than six cookies on each baking sheet.)

Bake for 14 to 18 minutes, until the cookies are firm around the edges and golden brown. (If the cookies are very large, they may need to bake for 1 to 2 minutes longer.) Let cool on the baking sheets for 5 minutes. Carefully remove the cookies from the baking sheets and put them on a cooling rack. Let cool to room temperature before serving.

Stored in a sealed container, the cookies will keep for 4 days at room temperature or 3 months in the freezer.

Per cookie: 278 calories, 3 g protein, 14 g fat (5 g sat), 39 g carbs, 203 mg sodium, 36 mg calcium, 3 g fiber

Macadamia nuts make two separate appearances in these bakery-style cookies. Salted, dry-roasted macadamias are the perfect counterpart to homemade macadamia gobs, a confection made from sweetened macadamia butter.

Double-Macadamia COOKIES

FREE OF: PEANUTS, YEAST   YIELD: 18 LARGE COOKIES

MACADAMIA GOBS
(prepare at least 2 hours in advance)

½ cup creamy macadamia butter, stirred well

6 tablespoons confectioners' sugar, sifted

½ teaspoon vanilla extract

MACADAMIA COOKIES

3 tablespoons warm water

1 tablespoon ground flaxseeds

¾ cup sorghum flour

¼ cup quinoa flour

¼ cup tapioca flour

½ teaspoon xanthan gum

½ teaspoon baking soda

¾ cup unrefined cane sugar

½ cup vegan buttery spread

1 teaspoon vanilla extract

Heaping ½ cup salted, dry-roasted macadamia nuts (see tip)

To make the macadamia gobs, line a plate or cutting board with waxed paper. Free a spot in the freezer so you can freeze the macadamia gobs later.

Put the macadamia butter in a small bowl. Add the confectioners' sugar and vanilla extract. Mix well. For each macadamia gob, scoop out 1 rounded teaspoon of the mixture and roll it into a very small ball between the palms of your hands. Put the ball on the waxed paper. Repeat with the remaining mixture. Put in the freezer for at least 2 hours, until the gobs are firm or almost firm.

To make the cookies, preheat the oven to 350 degrees F. Line a baking sheet with parchment paper or a silicone baking mat.

Put the water in a small bowl or measuring cup. Stir in the flaxseeds and let stand until thickened, about 5 minutes.

Put the sorghum flour, quinoa flour, tapioca flour, xanthan gum, and baking soda in a medium bowl. Stir with a dry whisk until combined.

Put the sugar and vegan buttery spread in the bowl of a stand mixer, with the paddle attachment, or a large bowl. Using the stand mixer or a hand mixer, beat on medium-high speed until fluffy, about 2 minutes. Add the flaxseed mixture and vanilla extract. Beat until well combined.

Turn the mixer to low speed. Gradually add the flour mixture to the sugar mixture, beating until just combined. Turn off the mixer. Carefully stir in the macadamia nuts and macadamia gobs, taking care not to smash the macadamia gobs.

For each cookie, scoop out 2 rounded tablespoons of dough and drop it onto the lined baking sheet. Repeat with the remaining dough, leaving 2 inches between cookies for spreading.

Per cookie: 196 calories, 2 g protein, 13 g fat (3 g sat), 19 g carbs, 73 mg sodium, 9 mg calcium, 2 g fiber

Bake for 10 to 12 minutes, until the cookies are firm around the edges and golden brown. (If the cookies are very large, they may need to bake for 1 to 2 minutes longer.) Let cool on the baking sheet for 5 minutes. Carefully remove the cookies from the baking sheet and put them on a cooling rack. Let cool to room temperature before serving.

Stored in a sealed container, the cookies will keep for 3 days at room temperature or 3 months in the freezer.

TIP: If you are only able to find unsalted macadamia nuts, add ⅛ teaspoon of salt to the flour mixture.

These cookies go by many names, including kitchen sink cookies and ranger cookies, but I think my name is to the point: these cookies have a little bit of everything. One bite, and your mouth will explode in a riot of texture and flavor.

A-Little-Bit-of-Everything COOKIES

FREE OF: LEGUMES, PEANUTS, YEAST

YIELD: 18 LARGE COOKIES

¼ cup warm water

1½ tablespoons ground flaxseeds

⅔ cup sorghum flour

½ cup teff flour

⅓ cup tapioca flour

2 teaspoons ground cinnamon

1 teaspoon xanthan gum

1 teaspoon baking soda

½ teaspoon baking powder

½ teaspoon fine sea salt

1¼ cups unrefined cane sugar

½ cup plus 2 tablespoons coconut oil, softened (see page 18)

2 teaspoons vanilla extract

1 cup creamy buckwheat cereal, uncooked (see page 15)

1 cup pecans, toasted (see sidebar, page 13) and chopped

¾ cup nondairy semisweet chocolate chips

¾ cup raisins, dried cranberries, or dried cherries, or a combination

½ cup unsweetened finely shredded dried coconut

Preheat the oven to 350 degrees F. Line a baking sheet with parchment paper or a silicone baking mat.

Put the water in a small bowl or measuring cup. Stir in the flaxseeds and let stand until thickened, about 5 minutes.

Put the sorghum flour, teff flour, tapioca flour, cinnamon, xanthan gum, baking soda, baking powder, and salt in a medium bowl. Stir with a dry whisk until combined.

Put the sugar and coconut oil in the bowl of a stand mixer, with the paddle attachment, or a large bowl. Using the stand mixer or a hand mixer, beat on medium-high speed until creamy, about 2 minutes. Mix well. Add the flaxseed mixture and vanilla extract. Beat until well combined.

Turn the mixer to medium speed. Gradually add the flour mixture to the sugar mixture, beating until combined. Add the buckwheat cereal and mix well. Turn off the mixer. Stir in the pecans, chocolate chips, raisins, and coconut until evenly distributed, using your hands if necessary.

For each cookie, scoop out ¼ rounded cup of dough. Use damp hands to roll the dough into a ball about the size of a golf ball. Put the ball on the lined baking sheet. Use damp fingers to press the dough until it's about ½ inch thick. If the dough is a bit crumbly, just squeeze it together with your hands. Repeat with the remaining dough, leaving at least 2 inches between cookies for spreading.

Bake for 13 to 16 minutes, until the tops of the cookies are firm and the edges are golden brown. Let cool on the baking sheet for 5 minutes. Carefully remove the cookies from the baking sheet and put them on a cooling rack. Let cool to room temperature before serving.

Stored in a sealed container, the cookies will keep for 4 days at room temperature or 3 months in the freezer.

TIP: Mix and match the pecans with other nuts or seeds and the raisins with other dried fruit to make these cookies exactly how you love them.

Per cookie: 314 calories, 4 g protein, 17 g fat (11 g sat), 41 g carbs, 141 mg sodium, 44 mg calcium, 4 g fiber

These soft, chewy cookies have just the right amount of spice and a hint of orange. Just be sure to remove the zest before juicing the orange.

Orange Spice COOKIES

FREE OF: LEGUMES, NUTS, PEANUTS, SEEDS, YEAST

YIELD: 18 COOKIES

¾ cup unrefined cane sugar

½ cup coconut oil, softened
(see page 18)

¼ cup pure maple syrup
(grade A or B)

2 tablespoons freshly squeezed
orange juice (remove the zest from
the orange before squeezing it)

1 teaspoon vanilla extract

1¼ cups sorghum flour

¼ cup quinoa flour

¼ cup tapioca flour

¾ teaspoon baking soda

¾ teaspoon xanthan gum

½ teaspoon fine sea salt

½ teaspoon ground cardamom

½ teaspoon ground cinnamon

¼ teaspoon ground ginger

¼ teaspoon ground nutmeg

1 tablespoon finely grated orange
zest (about 1 orange)

Preheat the oven to 350 degrees F. Line a baking sheet with parchment paper or a silicone baking mat.

Put the sugar, coconut oil, maple syrup, orange juice, and vanilla extract in the bowl of a stand mixer, with the paddle attachment, or a large bowl. Using the stand mixer or a hand mixer, beat on medium-high speed until smooth and creamy, about 2 minutes.

Put the sorghum flour, quinoa flour, tapioca flour, baking soda, xanthan gum, salt, cardamom, cinnamon, ginger, and nutmeg in a medium bowl. Stir with a dry whisk until combined. Add the orange zest and mix well.

Turn the mixer to low speed. Gradually add the flour mixture to the sugar mixture, beating until a soft dough forms.

For each cookie, scoop out 1 rounded tablespoon of dough and drop it onto the lined baking sheet. Repeat with the remaining dough, leaving about 2 inches between cookies for spreading.

Bake for 10 to 12 minutes, until the edges are firm and golden brown. (For a softer cookie, bake for about 10 minutes; for a firmer cookie, bake for 12 minutes.) Let cool on the baking sheet for 5 minutes. Carefully remove the cookies from the baking sheet and put them on a cooling rack. Let cool to room temperature before serving.

Stored in a sealed container, the cookies will keep for 3 days at room temperature or 3 months in the freezer.

Per cookie: 142 calories, 1 g protein, 7 g fat (6 g sat), 21 g carbs, 117 mg sodium, 2 mg calcium, 1 g fiber

You'll find the classic combination of mint and chocolate in these cookies, which are a little like brownies. Around the holidays, this recipe provides the perfect opportunity to use up candy canes; at other times, any hard mint candies will do.

MINT-BROWNIE Icebox COOKIES

FREE OF: NUTS, PEANUTS, YEAST

YIELD: 26 COOKIES

6 tablespoons strongly brewed coffee, warm (see tip, page 39)

2 tablespoons ground flaxseeds

¾ cup unsweetened cocoa powder, sifted

½ cup sorghum flour

¼ cup teff flour

¼ cup arrowroot starch

1 teaspoon xanthan gum

1 teaspoon baking powder

¼ teaspoon fine sea salt

Scant 1 cup unrefined cane sugar

¼ cup vegan buttery spread, at room temperature

1 teaspoon vanilla extract

½ teaspoon peppermint extract

4 candy canes, crushed, or ½ cup crushed hard mint candies (optional; see tip, page 86)

Put the coffee in a small bowl or measuring cup. Stir in the flaxseeds. Let stand until thickened, about 5 minutes.

Put the cocoa powder, sorghum flour, teff flour, arrowroot starch, xanthan gum, baking powder, and salt in a medium bowl. Stir with a dry whisk until combined.

Put the sugar and vegan buttery spread in a heavy-duty stand mixer, with the paddle attachment, or a large bowl. Using the stand mixer or a hand mixer, beat until smooth and fluffy, about 2 minutes. Add the flaxseed mixture, vanilla extract, and peppermint extract. Beat until well combined.

Turn the mixer to low speed. Gradually add the flour mixture to the sugar mixture, mixing until well combined. Stop occasionally to scrape down the bowl with a rubber spatula if necessary. The dough will be sticky.

Put a large piece of plastic wrap on a flat surface. Scrape the dough onto the plastic wrap using a rubber spatula. Cover with a second piece of plastic wrap and form the dough into a log, about 2 inches in diameter. Wrap the dough tightly in the plastic wrap. Refrigerate for at least 2 hours, until firm.

Preheat the oven to 350 degrees F. Line two baking sheets with parchment paper or silicone baking mats.

Remove the dough from the refrigerator. Unwrap the dough and put it on a cutting board. Cut the dough into ¼-inch slices using a serrated knife. Put the slices on the lined baking sheets, leaving about 1 inch between cookies for spreading. Sprinkle each slice with the optional crushed candy canes, lightly pressing the pieces into the dough.

Bake for 12 to 15 minutes, until the cookies are slightly firm to the touch. Let cool on the baking sheets for 5 minutes. Carefully remove the cookies from the baking sheets and put them on a cooling rack. Let cool to room temperature before serving.

Stored in a sealed container, the cookies will keep for 3 days at room temperature or 3 months in the freezer.

Brownie Icebox Cookies: Omit the peppermint extract and candy canes and use ½ teaspoon additional vanilla extract.

Per cookie: 67 calories, 1 g protein, 2 g fat (1 g sat), 12 g carbs, 49 mg sodium, 13 mg calcium, 2 g fiber

Made with buckwheat, these taste like **classic oatmeal raisin** cookies, but without the oats. Crunchy, chewy, and studded with raisins, this new version will surely become one of your favorites.

Noatmeal RAISIN COOKIES

FREE OF: PEANUTS, NUTS, YEAST   YIELD: 20 COOKIES

3 tablespoons warm water

2 tablespoons ground flaxseeds

½ cup vegan buttery spread, softened

⅔ cup unrefined cane sugar

2 teaspoons vanilla extract

¼ cup sorghum flour

¼ cup tapioca flour

¼ cup teff flour

½ teaspoon baking soda

½ teaspoon xanthan gum

½ teaspoon ground cinnamon

¼ teaspoon fine sea salt

1½ cups creamy buckwheat cereal, uncooked (see page 15)

⅔ cup raisins

Preheat the oven to 350 degrees F. Line two baking sheets with parchment paper or silicone baking mats.

Put the water in a small bowl or measuring cup. Stir in the flaxseeds and let stand until thickened, about 5 minutes.

Put the vegan buttery spread in the bowl of a stand mixer, with the paddle attachment, or a large bowl. Using the stand mixer or a hand mixer, beat on medium-high speed until creamy and fluffy, about 2 minutes. Add the sugar and mix well. Add the flaxseed mixture and vanilla extract. Beat until well combined.

Put the sorghum flour, tapioca flour, teff flour, baking soda, xanthan gum, cinnamon, and salt in a medium bowl. Stir with a dry whisk until combined.

Turn the mixer to medium speed. Gradually add the flour mixture to the sugar mixture, beating until well combined. Add the buckwheat cereal and mix well. Turn off the mixer. Stir in the raisins until evenly distributed.

For each cookie, scoop out 1 rounded tablespoon of dough and drop it onto a lined baking sheet. Press down lightly with a damp palm. Repeat with the remaining dough, leaving about 2 inches between cookies for spreading.

Bake for 12 to 14 minutes, until the edges are firm and golden brown. For a bit of extra crunch around the edges, bake 1 to 2 minutes longer. Let cool on the baking sheets for 10 minutes. Carefully remove the cookies from the baking sheets and put them on a cooling rack. Let cool to room temperature before serving.

Stored in a sealed container, the cookies will keep for 4 days at room temperature or 3 months in the freezer.

Per cookie: 144 calories, 2 g protein, 5 g fat (1 g sat), 24 g carbs, 42 mg sodium, 20 mg calcium, 2 g fiber

Before my gluten- and dairy-free days, one of my **favorite treats** was chocolate-covered raisins. Their memory inspired these cookies: **soft, fudgy** morsels dotted with chocolate chips and chewy raisins.

Double-Chocolate COOKIES WITH RAISINS

FREE OF: LEGUMES, NUTS, PEANUTS, YEAST   YIELD: 24 COOKIES

¼ cup warm water

1 tablespoon ground flaxseeds

1 cup sorghum flour

¾ cup unsweetened cocoa powder, sifted

½ cup teff flour

½ cup tapioca flour

1 teaspoon baking soda

1 teaspoon xanthan gum

½ teaspoon fine sea salt

1⅓ cups unrefined cane sugar

¾ cup coconut oil, melted

¼ cup nondairy milk

2 teaspoons vanilla extract

½ cup nondairy semisweet chocolate chips

¾ cup raisins

Preheat the oven to 350 degrees F. Line two baking sheets with parchment paper or silicone baking mats.

Put the water in a small bowl or measuring cup. Stir in the flaxseeds and let stand until thickened, about 5 minutes.

Put the sorghum flour, cocoa powder, teff flour, tapioca flour, baking soda, xanthan gum, and salt in a medium bowl. Stir with a dry whisk until combined.

Put the sugar and coconut oil in a large bowl. Stir briskly with a whisk until smooth and creamy, about 2 minutes. Alternatively, use a stand mixer, with the paddle attachment, or a hand mixer. Add the flaxseed mixture, nondairy milk, and vanilla extract. Mix until well combined.

Add the flour mixture to the sugar mixture. Mix well. Stir in the chocolate chips and raisins until evenly distributed. The dough will seem very oily.

For each cookie, scoop 1 heaping tablespoon of dough into your hand. Roll into a ball between the palms of your hands. Put the ball on a lined baking sheet. Use your palm to slightly flatten the cookie. Repeat with the remaining dough.

Bake for 11 to 14 minutes, just until the edges begin to firm for a soft cookie or until the center is firm for a harder cookie. Let cool on the baking sheets for 10 minutes. Carefully remove the cookies from the baking sheets and put them on a cooling rack. Let cool to room temperature before serving. The cookies will soften as they sit.

Stored in a sealed container, the cookies will keep for 3 days at room temperature or 3 months in the freezer.

Per cookie: 186 calories, 2 g protein, 10 g fat (8 g sat), 27 g carbs, 101 mg sodium, 22 mg calcium, 2 g fiber

When it comes to peanut butter cookies, we all have our favorites. To me, a *really good* peanut butter cookie has *crispy edges* and a *chewy center,* and that's why I think these are the best.

REALLY GOOD Peanut Butter COOKIES

FREE OF: NUTS, SEEDS, YEAST

YIELD: 12 LARGE COOKIES

½ cup creamy or crunchy natural peanut butter

½ cup light agave nectar

3 tablespoons canola oil

1 tablespoon nondairy milk

1 teaspoon vanilla extract

⅓ cup sorghum flour

⅓ cup teff flour

⅓ cup arrowroot starch

2 tablespoons unrefined cane sugar

½ teaspoon baking powder

½ teaspoon baking soda

½ teaspoon xanthan gum

⅛ teaspoon fine sea salt

Preheat the oven to 350 degrees F. Line a baking sheet with parchment paper or silicone baking mats.

Put the peanut butter and agave nectar in the bowl of a stand mixer, with the paddle attachment, or a large bowl. Using the stand mixer or a hand mixer, beat on medium-high speed until creamy and well mixed, about 2 minutes. Add the oil, nondairy milk, and vanilla extract. Beat until smooth and well combined.

Put the sorghum flour, teff flour, arrowroot starch, sugar, baking powder, baking soda, xanthan gum, and salt in a small bowl. Stir with a dry whisk until combined. Turn the mixer to medium speed. Gradually add the flour mixture to the peanut butter mixture, beating until combined. Turn off the mixer. The dough will seem oily.

For each cookie, scoop 1 heaping tablespoon of dough into your hand. Roll into a ball between the palms of your hands. Put the ball on the lined baking sheet. Repeat with the remaining dough.

Use your palm to slightly flatten each ball. Press a crisscross pattern into the top of each cookie with a fork.

Bake for 7 to 8 minutes, just until the edges begin to firm. Let cool on the baking sheet for 5 minutes. Carefully remove the cookies from the baking sheet and put them on a cooling rack. Let cool to room temperature before serving.

Stored in a sealed container, the cookies will keep for 3 days at room temperature or 3 months in the freezer.

Nondairy Ice-Cream Sandwiches: Scoop about ⅓ cup of slightly softened nondairy ice cream onto a cookie. Press a second cookie on top. Roll the exposed ice cream in nondairy semisweet chocolate chips. Wrap tightly and freeze for about 30 minutes before serving.

Chocolate Chip–Peanut Butter Cookies: Add ½ cup of nondairy semisweet chocolate chips to the flour mixture.

Per cookie: 178 calories, 4 g protein, 8 g fat (1 g sat), 23 g carbs, 89 mg sodium, 14 mg calcium, 2 g fiber

If you love chocolate-hazelnut spread, you'll adore these fudgy thumbprints. Raspberry jam adds just the right amount of tanginess, while the chocolate drizzle delivers a bit of decadence.

CHOCOLATE-HAZELNUT-RASPBERRY Thumbprints

FREE OF: PEANUTS, SEEDS, YEAST

YIELD: 30 COOKIES

½ cup unrefined cane sugar

¼ cup vegan buttery spread

½ cup roasted hazelnut butter

1 teaspoon vanilla extract

⅔ cup sorghum flour

⅓ cup teff flour

⅓ cup tapioca flour

¾ teaspoon baking powder

½ teaspoon xanthan gum

¼ teaspoon fine sea salt

2 tablespoons nondairy milk, plus more as needed

3 tablespoons fruit-sweetened raspberry jam, plus more as needed

¼ cup nondairy semisweet chocolate chips

Preheat the oven to 375 degrees F. Line a baking sheet with parchment paper or a silicone baking mat.

Put the sugar and vegan buttery spread in the bowl of a stand mixer, with the paddle attachment, or a large bowl. Using the stand mixer or a hand mixer, beat on medium-high speed until creamy and well mixed, about 2 minutes. Add the hazelnut butter and vanilla extract. Beat until smooth and well mixed.

Put the sorghum flour, teff flour, tapioca flour, baking powder, xanthan gum, and salt in a small bowl. Stir with a dry whisk until combined. Turn the mixer to medium speed. Gradually add the flour mixture to the hazelnut butter mixture, beating until well combined. Add the nondairy milk, about 1 tablespoon at a time, until the mixture is smooth. Test the mixture by squeezing a small amount in your hand: it should stick together easily. If necessary, add up to 1 tablespoon additional nondairy milk, 1 teaspoon at a time, until the desired consistency is achieved. Turn off the mixer.

For each cookie, scoop 1 heaping tablespoon of dough into your hand. Roll into a ball between the palms of your hands. Put the ball on the lined baking sheet. Repeat with the remaining dough.

Gently press your finger into the center of each ball. If the edges of the ball crack, use your fingers to reshape the dough around the indentation. Spoon about ¼ teaspoon of the jam into each indentation.

Bake for 10 to 12 minutes, until the edges are firm. Let cool on the baking sheet for 10 minutes. Carefully remove the cookies from the baking sheet and put them on a cooling rack.

Per cookie: 98 calories, 1 g protein, 5 g fat (1 g sat), 14 g carbs, 40 mg sodium, 19 mg calcium, 1 g fiber

Put the chocolate chips in a microwave-safe bowl. Microwave on high for 15 seconds and stir. Repeat as needed until the chocolate has melted. To melt the chocolate on the stovetop, fill a small saucepan with one inch of water. Bring to a simmer over medium heat. Put a glass bowl on top of the saucepan, making sure it doesn't touch the water but creates a seal to trap the steam produced by the simmering water. Put the chocolate chips in the bowl. As the bowl heats, the chocolate will begin to melt. Stir occasionally, until the chocolate is completely melted. Let cool for 5 minutes.

Scrape the melted chocolate into a small ziplock bag using a rubber spatula. Snip off a very tiny piece of one of the bag's bottom corners using scissors. Squeeze the bag to drizzle a bit of the melted chocolate in a zigzag pattern over each cookie. Let the chocolate and cookies cool to room temperature before serving.

Stored in a sealed container, the cookies will keep for 3 days in the refrigerator or 3 months in the freezer.

The tart dried cherries and bitter cacao nibs provide a **unique balance of flavor** in these shortbread cookies.

Shortbread WITH DRIED CHERRIES AND CACAO NIBS

FREE OF: LEGUMES, NUTS, PEANUTS, SEEDS, YEAST   YIELD: 30 SHORTBREAD

¾ cup sorghum flour

½ cup cornstarch

¼ cup quinoa flour

2 tablespoons tapioca flour

¾ teaspoon xanthan gum

¼ teaspoon fine sea salt

½ cup confectioners' sugar, sifted

½ cup coconut oil, melted

2 tablespoons chopped dried cherries, packed

1½ tablespoons cacao nibs

Put the sorghum flour, cornstarch, quinoa flour, tapioca flour, xanthan gum, and salt in the bowl of a stand mixer, with the paddle attachment, or a large bowl. Stir with a dry whisk until combined. Add the confectioners' sugar and mix well.

Turn the stand mixer or a hand mixer on medium speed. Add the coconut oil to the flour mixture. Mix until well combined. Add the cherries and cacao nibs. Mix until evenly distributed. The dough will seem very wet.

Scrape the dough into a large ziplock bag using a rubber spatula. Push the dough to the bottom of the bag. Use a rolling pin to roll the dough in the bag until it's a rectangle, about ¼ inch thick. (The important thing is to have a solid rectangle of dough that is ¼ inch thick; depending on the size of the bag you use, the dough may or may not fill the bag completely.)

While the dough is still in the bag, put it on a cutting board. Put the dough and the cutting board in the freezer for about 20 minutes or in the refrigerator for about 40 minutes until the dough is firm but not rock hard.

Preheat the oven to 325 degrees F. Line two baking sheets with parchment paper or silicone baking mats.

Remove the dough from the freezer or refrigerator. Cut the bag open on all sides using sharp scissors. Remove the bag and put the hardened dough directly on the cutting board. Cut the dough with a very sharp knife into 2 x 1-inch rectangles. If the dough crumbles, let it sit at room temperature for about 10 minutes before trying again. (Don't let the dough become too soft; it should only be soft enough to cut easily with a sharp knife.) Put the rectangles on the baking sheets.

Per shortbread: 70 calories, 1 g protein, 4 g fat (3 g sat), 8 g carbs, 19 mg sodium, 2 mg calcium, 1 g fiber

Bake for 16 to 22 minutes, until golden brown on the edges. Let cool on the baking sheets for 5 minutes. Carefully remove the cookies from the baking sheets and put them on a cooling rack. Let cool to room temperature before serving.

Stored in a sealed container, the shortbread will keep for 4 days at room temperature or 3 months in the freezer.

TIP: Instead of using the ziplock bag, you can make similar (though slightly thicker) cookies by spreading the dough in a pan instead. After you prepare the dough, line an 8-inch square pan with parchment paper, leaving a few inches of the paper hanging over the edges on opposite ends for easy removal. Scrape the dough into the pan using a rubber spatula. Spread evenly. Put in the freezer or refrigerator as directed. Remove from the freezer or refrigerator and lift the dough out of the pan using the edges of the parchment paper. Put the dough on the cutting board. Cut into rectangles as directed. Bake for about 25 minutes, until golden brown.

These cookies don't really twist apart, they're not very crunchy, and they don't have any trans fats. But the differences between these Noreos and their commercial counterpart are exactly what make them **so wonderful.**

NOREOS Chocolate Sandwich COOKIES

FREE OF: NUTS, PEANUTS, YEAST   YIELD: 24 SANDWICH COOKIES

CHOCOLATE COOKIES

2 tablespoons warm water

1½ tablespoons ground flaxseeds

¾ cup vegan buttery spread

1 cup confectioners' sugar, sifted

6 tablespoons unsweetened cocoa powder, sifted

1 tablespoon nondairy milk

1 teaspoon vanilla extract

½ cup sorghum flour

½ cup teff flour

½ cup tapioca flour, plus more for rolling

1½ teaspoons xanthan gum

⅛ teaspoon baking powder

⅛ teaspoon fine sea salt

VANILLA FILLING

1 tablespoon water, plus more as needed

2 teaspoons arrowroot starch

¼ teaspoon vanilla extract

2 cups confectioners' sugar, sifted, plus more for kneading

To make the cookies, put the water in a small bowl or measuring cup. Stir in the flaxseeds and let stand until thickened, about 5 minutes.

Put the vegan buttery spread in the bowl of a stand mixer, with the paddle attachment, or a large bowl. Using the stand mixer or a hand mixer, beat until smooth and fluffy, about 2 minutes. Turn the speed to low. Gradually add the confectioners' sugar and cocoa powder, mixing until combined. Add the flaxseed mixture, nondairy milk, and vanilla extract. Mix well.

Put the sorghum flour, teff flour, tapioca flour, xanthan gum, baking powder, and salt in a medium bowl. Stir with a dry whisk until combined. Turn the mixer to low speed. Gradually add the flour mixture to the sugar mixture, mixing until well combined.

Put a large piece of plastic wrap on a flat surface. Scrape the dough onto the plastic wrap using a rubber spatula and form it into a ball. Wrap the dough tightly in the plastic wrap. Refrigerate for 30 minutes.

Preheat the oven to 325 degrees F. Line a baking sheet with parchment paper or a silicone baking mat.

Remove the dough from the refrigerator. Unwrap the dough and put it on a lightly floured surface. Roll the dough with a lightly floured rolling pin until it's ⅛ to ¼ inch thick (the thinner you roll the dough, the crispier the cookies will be). The dough may seem very oily, but don't add additional flour. Cut the rolled dough using a 1½- to 2-inch round cookie cutter. With a thin metal spatula or butter knife, transfer the cookies to the lined baking sheet. Repeat with the remaining dough, rerolling the scraps as needed. If the dough becomes too soft, wrap it in plastic wrap and put it in the freezer for about 10 minutes.

Bake for 12 to 15 minutes, until the cookies are slightly firm to the touch. Let cool on the baking sheet for about 7 minutes, until firm. Carefully remove the cookies from the baking sheet and put them on a cooling rack. Let cool while you prepare the filling (save the lined baking

Per sandwich cookie: 145 calories, 1 g protein, 6 g fat (2 g sat), 22 g carbs, 63 mg sodium, 8 mg calcium, 1 g fiber

sheet to use when you make the filling). The cookies should be completely cool before they are filled.

To make the filling, put 1 tablespoon of the water and the arrowroot starch and the vanilla extract in a large bowl. Whisk until smooth. Add the confectioners' sugar, about ½ cup at a time, stirring until smooth. Add additional water, about 1 teaspoon at a time, if necessary, until the mixture holds together and is very firm and pliable. When the mixture is firm, transfer it to a flat surface sprinkled with additional confectioners' sugar. Knead until smooth. The filling should be the consistency of firm pastry dough. Cover the filling with a moist towel to prevent it from drying out.

To assemble the cookies, scoop about 1 tablespoon of the filling into your hand and roll it into a ball between your palms. Put the ball on the lined baking sheet you used to make the cookies (the baking sheet must be cool). Repeat with the remaining filling. Flatten each ball between your palms to create a ¼-inch thick circle the same size as the cookies.

Gently press the filling between the bottom sides of two cookies. (If the filling doesn't stick to the cookies, remove the filling and use your finger to lightly dampen both sides with water. Press the filling between the two cookies once again.) Repeat with the remaining filling and cookies.

Stored in a sealed container, the cookies will keep for 3 days at room temperature or 1 month in the freezer. These cookies taste good right after they are made, but they taste even better after a few hours or the next day.

TIPS

- Count the cookies before making the filling. For example, if you have 48 cookies, divide the filling into 24 portions so no filling is left over after you assemble the sandwich cookies.

- You can double the recipe and freeze these cookies; they will be softer after they have been frozen and thawed.

VARIATION: For mint filling, replace the ¼ teaspoon of vanilla extract with ¼ teaspoon of peppermint extract.

Up here in Canada, we're known for more than just our Nanaimo Bars (page 112). Cream-Filled Maple Leaf Cookies, another popular commodity, showcase the bounty of the country's many maple farms. If you've never had one, now's the time to enjoy this sandwich cookie filled with maple buttercream frosting.

Cream-Filled MAPLE LEAF COOKIES

FREE OF: NUTS, PEANUTS, YEAST   YIELD: 24 LARGE SANDWICH COOKIES

MAPLE LEAF COOKIES

2 cups plus
    2 tablespoons
    sorghum flour

½ cup quinoa flour

½ cup tapioca flour,
    plus more for
    rolling

1½ teaspoons
    xanthan gum

½ teaspoon fine
    sea salt

1 cup vegan buttery
    spread

Heaping ¾ cup
    maple sugar

½ cup pure maple
    syrup (grade B;
    see tip)

1 tablespoon
    nondairy milk

2 teaspoons ground
    flaxseeds

Per sandwich cookie: 232
calories, 2 g protein, 12 g
fat (3 g sat), 31 g carbs, 153
mg sodium, 2 mg calcium,
1 g fiber

To make the cookies, put the sorghum flour, quinoa flour, tapioca flour, xanthan gum, and salt in a medium bowl. Stir with a dry whisk until combined.

Put the vegan buttery spread and maple sugar in the bowl of a stand mixer, with the paddle attachment, or a large bowl. Using the stand mixer or a hand mixer, beat until smooth and fluffy, about 2 minutes. Turn the mixer to low speed. Continue to beat while adding the maple syrup in a steady stream. Add the nondairy milk and flaxseeds. Beat until well combined, occasionally stopping to scrape down the bowl with a rubber spatula if necessary.

With the mixer still on low speed, gradually add the flour mixture to the maple sugar mixture, beating until well combined. The dough will be very soft. Turn off the mixer.

Divide the dough into two portions. Put two sheets of plastic wrap on a flat surface. Scrape the first portion of dough onto one sheet of plastic wrap using a rubber spatula and form it into a ball. Wrap the dough tightly in the plastic wrap. Repeat with the remaining dough and plastic wrap. Refrigerate for at least 2 hours.

Preheat the oven to 350 degrees F. Line two baking sheets with parchment paper or silicone baking mats.

Remove one portion of the dough from the refrigerator (keep the other portion in the refrigerator). Unwrap the dough and put it on a lightly floured surface. Roll the dough with a lightly floured rolling pin until it's ⅛ to ¼ inch thick (the thinner you roll the dough, the crispier the cookies will be). Cut the rolled dough using a cookie cutter shaped like a maple leaf. Transfer the cookies to a lined baking sheet using a thin metal spatula or butter knife (12 to 15 cookies will fit on one baking sheet). Leftover scraps of dough will be too soft to reroll; rewrap the scraps in the plastic wrap and put them in the freezer for 10 to 15 minutes before rerolling.

Refrigerate the unbaked cookies on the baking sheet for 10 minutes. Bake for 12 to 15 minutes, until the cookies are browned on the edges and slightly firm to the touch. Let cool on the baking sheet for about 5 minutes, until firm. Carefully remove the cookies from the baking sheet and put them on a cooling rack.

Repeat until all the dough has been rolled, cut, and baked (this should take four or five rounds). Let the cookies cool completely before you prepare the frosting.

MAPLE BUTTERCREAM FROSTING

½ cup vegan buttery spread

2 cups confectioners' sugar, sifted, plus more as needed

2 tablespoons pure maple syrup (grade B; see tip)

¾ teaspoon maple extract

To make the frosting, put the vegan buttery spread in the bowl of a stand mixer, with the paddle attachment, or a large bowl. Using the stand mixer or a hand mixer, beat until fluffy, about 2 minutes. Add 1 cup of the confectioners' sugar. Beat until smooth. Add the maple syrup, maple extract, and the remaining cup of confectioners' sugar. Continue to beat until smooth and well combined, about 2 more minutes. If the frosting is too thin, add more confectioners' sugar, 1 tablespoon at a time, until the desired consistency is achieved.

To assemble the cookies, put 1 heaping tablespoon of frosting on the bottom of a cookie and spread the frosting evenly using a butter knife or spreader. Press a second cookie, bottom-side down, on top of the frosting. Repeat with the remaining cookies and frosting.

Stored in a sealed container, the cookies will keep for 3 days at room temperature or 1 month in the freezer. These cookies taste good right after they are made, but they taste even better after a few hours or the next day.

TIPS

- Use grade B maple syrup (see page 11) to give these cookies a strong maple flavor; grade A maple syrup is too mild for this recipe. If you don't have grade B maple syrup and must use grade A, add ½ teaspoon of maple extract to the cookie dough when you add the nondairy milk and flaxseeds. Also add ½ teaspoon of additional maple extract to the frosting. The dough and frosting can both be adjusted to taste.

- If you want the cookies to have the detailed look of a veined maple leaf, use the tip of a butter knife to create shallow indents (veins) in the cookie after it's cut out and before it's baked.

- As an alternative to spreading the frosting on the cookies with a butter knife, use a cake-decorating bag to pipe the frosting onto the cookies. Start by piping around the edge of a cookie, then fill in the center.

- Any leftover frosting can be frozen and used to frost cupcakes, such as French Toast Cupcakes (page 70).

A **holiday favorite,** these soft cutout cookies are everyone's top pick, including mine. They are the first treat I reach for on the cookie tray.

TRADITIONAL Gingerbread Men

FREE OF: NUTS, PEANUTS, SEEDS   YIELD: ABOUT 36 COOKIES, DEPENDING ON THE SIZE OF THE COOKIE CUTTER

GINGERBREAD COOKIES

1 1/4 cups sorghum flour

3/4 cup teff flour

3/4 cup tapioca flour, plus more for rolling

2 teaspoons ground ginger (see tip)

2 teaspoons ground cinnamon (see tip)

1 1/2 teaspoons xanthan gum

3/4 teaspoon baking powder

1/2 teaspoon baking soda

1/2 teaspoon ground nutmeg (see tip)

1/2 teaspoon fine sea salt

1/4 teaspoon ground cloves (see tip)

1/2 cup vegan buttery spread

1/2 cup unrefined cane sugar

1/2 cup light molasses

1 teaspoon vanilla extract

3 tablespoons nondairy milk

1 tablespoon cider vinegar

1 tablespoon ground flaxseeds

To make the cookies, put the sorghum flour, teff flour, tapioca flour, ginger, cinnamon, xanthan gum, baking powder, baking soda, nutmeg, salt, and cloves in a medium bowl. Stir with a dry whisk until combined.

Put the vegan buttery spread and sugar in the bowl of a stand mixer, with the paddle attachment, or a large bowl. Using the stand mixer or a hand mixer, beat on medium-high speed until fluffy, about 2 minutes. Turn the mixer to low speed. Add the molasses and vanilla extract. Beat until well combined. Add the nondairy milk, vinegar, and flaxseeds. Turn the mixer to medium speed. Beat until well combined.

Turn the mixer to low speed. Gradually add the flour mixture to the sugar mixture, beating until a soft dough forms. Turn off the mixer.

Divide the dough into four portions. Put four sheets of plastic wrap on a flat surface. Scrape the first portion of dough onto one sheet of plastic wrap using a rubber spatula and form it into a ball. Wrap the dough tightly in the plastic wrap. Repeat with the remaining dough and plastic wrap. Refrigerate for at least 6 hours.

Preheat the oven to 375 degrees F. Line two baking sheets with parchment paper or silicone baking mats.

Remove one portion of the dough from the refrigerator (keep the others in the refrigerator). Unwrap the dough and put it on a lightly floured surface. Roll the dough with a lightly floured rolling pin until it's 1/8 to 1/4 inch thick (the thinner you roll the dough, the crispier the cookies will be). Cut the dough using a cookie cutter shaped like a gingerbread man. Transfer the cookies to a lined baking sheet using a thin metal spatula or butter knife. Repeat with the remaining dough, rerolling the scraps as needed. If the dough becomes too soft, wrap it in plastic wrap and put it in the freezer for about 15 minutes.

Per cookie (based on 36 cookies): 90 calories, 1 g protein, 3 g fat (1 g sat), 16 g carbs, 79 mg sodium, 22 mg calcium, 1 g fiber

LEMON ICING

½ cup confectioners' sugar, sifted

1½ teaspoons cornstarch

2 teaspoons nondairy milk, plus more as needed

1 teaspoon freshly squeezed lemon juice (see tip)

Bake for 7 to 12 minutes (thicker cookies will take longer to bake), until lightly browned on the edges and slightly firm to the touch. Don't overbake the cookies or they will become dry. Let cool on the baking sheets for 5 minutes. Carefully remove the cookies from the baking sheets and put them on a cooling rack to cool completely before decorating or serving.

To make the icing, put the confectioners' sugar and cornstarch in a small bowl. Whisk until well combined. Add the nondairy milk and lemon juice. Mix well. Add up to 1 teaspoon additional nondairy milk, a little at a time, as needed to achieve a thick but spreadable consistency.

Scrape the icing into a small ziplock bag using a rubber spatula. Snip off a tiny piece of one of the bag's bottom corners using scissors. Squeeze the bag to push the icing through the hole. Decorate the cookies as desired. Let the cookies stand for at least 20 minutes to allow the icing to harden before serving or storing.

Stored in a sealed container, the cookies will keep for 3 days at room temperature or 3 months in the freezer.

TIPS

- If you love spicy gingerbread, feel free to use more spice than specified.
- The Lemon Icing hardens as it stands, making it perfect for decorating Traditional Gingerbread Men. This recipe makes enough icing to decorate the cookies simply; to decorate more intricately, double the icing recipe.
- Feel free to omit the lemon juice in the icing if you prefer a more neutral flavor.
- For a smaller yield of cookies, this recipe can be cut in half with the same results.

Bars, Squares, & Biscotti

No man in the world has more courage than the man who can stop after eating one peanut [butter and jam blondie].

ATTRIBUTED TO CHANNING POLLOCK, AMERICAN PLAYWRIGHT

See Peanut Butter and Jam Blondies, page 116.

ooey blondies and brownies, creamy layered confections, and crunchy biscotti are all terrific alternatives to the average cookie. Dressed up, bars and squares can be so much more than a sweet snack. They can easily be transformed into an elegant final course: simply serve a generous portion with a scoop of nondairy ice cream and a garnish of fresh fruit. This impromptu dessert is guaranteed to satisfy any dinner guest.

TIPS FOR BAKING THE BEST BARS AND SQUARES

- Use the exact pan the recipe calls for. Otherwise, the baking time may be affected, the size of the bars may be affected, and the bars may burn or turn out crumbly.
- Line the pan with a large sheet of aluminum foil or parchment paper, letting the excess hang over two opposite sides of the pan. After the contents are baked and cooled, remove them from the pan cleanly and easily by lifting out the foil or paper.
- When putting a crust in the pan to form a base, press it firmly and snugly into the pan. This will help prevent crumbling when you slice the bars.
- To ensure even baking, spread toppings in a uniform layer over the base.
- Check for doneness a few minutes early. Bars can easily overbake due to a number of factors, including the oven, baking pan, and ingredients.
- Let the contents of the pan cool completely before removing or slicing into bars or squares (no matter how tempted you may be).

TIPS FOR BAKING UNBEATABLE BISCOTTI

- Because biscotti dough is often very firm, stir in hard or chunky ingredients, such as chocolate chips, nuts, or dried fruit, by hand.
- Do not overbake. After the first baking, the biscotti loaves should be golden brown and firm but not hard.
- If you have a convection oven, consider using the convection setting when baking the biscotti for the second time. Put the biscotti directly on the oven racks (without a pan) to toast it quickly and efficiently.

| TABLE 9 | Troubleshooting when baking bars and squares |

PROBLEM	POSSIBLE CAUSES AND SOLUTIONS
The bars are baking too quickly or are overbaking.	Dark pans (which are often nonstick) and glass dishes absorb more heat and transfer it to the bars (see page 140 for pan recommendations). If using a dark pan or glass dish, decrease the oven temperature by 25 degrees F or decrease the baking time.
The bottom of the bars are burnt.	The bars were not baked in the center of the oven.
The bars are difficult to remove from the pan.	The pan was not well oiled or lined. If lining the pan with aluminum foil, press the foil so that it's smooth and snug in the pan.
The base of a layered bar crumbles.	The mixture may have been too dry. If the mixture doesn't stick together when you squeeze it in your hand, add a small amount of nondairy milk until the desired consistency is achieved.

These **delectable** squares have a flaky coconut base and a crunchy walnut and coconut topping. Let me warn you—you'll be **going back** for seconds.

Coconut-Walnut SQUARES

FREE OF: PEANUTS, YEAST   YIELD: 25 SMALL OR 16 MEDIUM SQUARES

COCONUT BASE

1 cup unsweetened finely shredded dried coconut

¾ cup sorghum flour

½ cup unrefined cane sugar

¼ cup tapioca flour

2 teaspoons baking powder

1¼ teaspoons xanthan gum

½ teaspoon ground cinnamon

¼ teaspoon fine sea salt

½ cup vegan buttery spread, melted

WALNUT-COCONUT TOPPING

6 tablespoons warm water

2 tablespoons ground flaxseeds

1 teaspoon vanilla extract

1 teaspoon butterscotch extract (optional)

1 cup unsweetened finely shredded dried coconut (see tip)

⅔ cup coarsely chopped walnuts, toasted (see sidebar, page 13)

½ cup unrefined cane sugar

1 tablespoon nondairy milk

To make the base, preheat the oven to 350 degrees F. Line an 8-inch square baking pan with aluminum foil, leaving a few inches of foil hanging over opposite sides of the pan. Lightly oil the foil.

Put the coconut, sorghum flour, sugar, tapioca flour, baking powder, xanthan gum, cinnamon, and salt in a large bowl. Stir with a dry whisk until combined. Gradually add the vegan buttery spread, stirring with a spoon until well incorporated.

Scrape the mixture into the lined pan using a rubber spatula. Press the mixture evenly into the pan using the back of a fork. Bake for 15 minutes. Remove from the oven but keep the oven on. Put the pan on a cooling rack while you prepare the topping.

To make the topping, put the water in a small bowl or measuring cup. Stir in the flaxseeds, vanilla extract, and optional butterscotch extract. Let stand until thickened, about 5 minutes. Put the coconut, walnuts, and sugar in a medium bowl. Add the flaxseed mixture and nondairy milk. Mix well. Scrape the topping onto the slightly cooled base using a rubber spatula. Spread evenly.

Bake for 15 minutes. Let cool completely in the pan.

To cut and serve, use the foil to lift the contents out of the pan. Put the contents on a plate or in a container. Slice into squares using a sharp knife.

Stored in a sealed container, the squares will keep for 3 days at room temperature or in the refrigerator or 3 months in the freezer.

TIP: For more coconut flavor, toast the coconut before adding it to the topping (see sidebar, page 13).

Chocolate-Coconut-Walnut Squares: Add about ½ cup of nondairy semisweet chocolate chips to the topping before baking.

Per square (based on 25 squares): 150 calories, 2 g protein, 10 g fat (5 g sat), 15 g carbs, 81 mg sodium, 22 mg calcium, 2 g fiber

Here is my rendition of the Canadian Nanaimo bar, which is typically rife with allergens and animal ingredients. This version nixes the gluten, drops the dairy, and forgoes the eggs. Packed with **nutritious** ingredients, this **tasty bar** can stand up to (and, dare I say, surpass) the original.

Canadian NANAIMO BARS

FREE OF: CORN,* PEANUTS, YEAST   YIELD: 20 BARS

CHOCOLATE-COCONUT BASE

3 tablespoons warm water

1 tablespoon ground flaxseeds

6 tablespoons vegan buttery spread

⅓ cup unsweetened cocoa powder, sifted

¼ cup unrefined cane sugar

1 tablespoon coconut oil

1¼ cups crushed gluten-free flaked cereal (see tip; *for corn-free, use a gluten-free cereal that is free of corn)

1 cup unsweetened finely shredded dried coconut

½ cup walnuts or almonds, toasted (see sidebar, page 13) and finely ground

CREAMY VANILLA FILLING

¼ cup vegan buttery spread, softened

3 tablespoons arrowroot starch

2 tablespoons nondairy milk

1 teaspoon vanilla extract

⅛ teaspoon turmeric (optional, for color)

2 cups confectioners' sugar, sifted

To make the base, line a 9-inch square baking pan with aluminum foil, leaving a few inches of foil hanging over opposite sides of the pan. Lightly oil the foil.

Put the water and flaxseeds in a medium saucepan. Cook over medium heat, until the mixture begins to thicken, about 2 minutes. Add the vegan buttery spread, cocoa powder, sugar, and coconut oil. Decrease the heat to medium-low and cook, stirring often, until smooth, about 2 minutes. Remove from the heat.

Put the cereal, coconut, and walnuts in a large bowl. Add the flaxseed mixture to the cereal mixture. Stir until well combined. Alternatively, use damp hands to combine, but be careful because the mixture will be hot. The mixture should stick together when you squeeze a portion of it in your hand.

Scrape the mixture into the lined pan using a rubber spatula. Press the mixture evenly into the pan using the back of a fork or your fingers. Put the pan in the freezer while you make the filling.

To make the filling, put the vegan buttery spread in the bowl of a stand mixer, with the paddle attachment, or a large bowl. Using the stand mixer or a hand mixer, beat on medium-high speed until smooth, about 2 minutes. Add the arrowroot starch, nondairy milk, vanilla extract, and optional turmeric. Beat to combine. Add the confectioners' sugar, about ½ cup at a time, and continue beating until the mixture is light and fluffy, 2 to 3 minutes.

Remove the pan from the freezer. Scrape the filling onto the base using a rubber spatula and spread evenly over the top of the base. Return the pan to the freezer.

Per bar: 235 calories, 2 g protein, 15 g fat (7 g sat), 26 g carbs, 74 mg sodium, 24 mg calcium, 2 g fiber

CHOCOLATE TOPPING

¾ cup nondairy semisweet chocolate chips

2 tablespoons vegan buttery spread

To make the topping, put the chocolate chips and vegan buttery spread in a small microwave-safe bowl. Microwave on high for 15 seconds and stir. Repeat as needed until the chocolate has melted and the mixture is smooth. To melt the chocolate on the stovetop, fill a small saucepan with one inch of water. Bring to a simmer over medium heat. Put a glass bowl on top of the saucepan, making sure it doesn't touch the water but creates a seal to trap the steam produced by the simmering water. Put the chocolate chips and vegan buttery spread in the bowl. As the bowl heats, the chocolate will begin to melt. Stir occasionally, until the chocolate is completely melted.

Remove the pan from the freezer. Spread the topping evenly over the filling using a metal offset spatula. Score the top into 20 bars using a sharp knife. This will make it easier to cut the bars and prevent the topping from cracking. Return the pan to the freezer for 10 minutes to firm the topping.

When the topping is firm, transfer the pan to the refrigerator. Refrigerate for at least 4 hours before serving.

To cut and serve, use the foil to lift the contents out of the pan. Put the contents on a plate or in a container. Dip a sharp knife into very hot water before slicing into bars to prevent the topping from cracking.

Stored in a sealed container, the bars will keep for 5 days in the refrigerator or 3 months in the freezer.

TIPS

- Crush the cereal until it's the consistency of graham cracker crumbs or ground nuts.
- The ingredients used in the base must be finely ground and well crushed. Otherwise, the base will be crumbly.

Chocolate-Mint Nanaimo Bars: Add 1 teaspoon of peppermint extract to the filling and omit the turmeric. For holiday flair, sprinkle crushed candy canes (see tip, page 86) over the chocolate topping before it sets.

What do you get when you combine a chewy almond butter base, a fudgy almond butter filling, candied almonds, and a hint of sea salt? Everything an almond butter lover has ever wanted.

TRIPLE-ALMOND Squares

FREE OF: LEGUMES, PEANUTS, SEEDS, YEAST   YIELD: 25 SMALL OR 16 MEDIUM SQUARES

ALMOND BUTTER BASE

¼ cup sorghum flour

2 tablespoons tapioca flour

2 tablespoons teff flour

¼ teaspoon xanthan gum

⅛ teaspoon fine sea salt

½ cup creamy roasted almond butter

⅓ cup light agave nectar

1 teaspoon vanilla extract

CANDIED ALMOND TOPPING

1 cup almonds

2 tablespoons light agave nectar

1 tablespoon unrefined cane sugar

½ teaspoon sea salt

FUDGY ALMOND BUTTER FILLING

1 cup plus 2 tablespoons creamy
   roasted almond butter

6 tablespoons light agave nectar

5 tablespoons coconut oil, melted

2 teaspoons vanilla extract

To make the base, preheat the oven to 350 degrees F. Line an 8-inch square baking pan with aluminum foil, leaving a few inches of foil hanging over opposite sides of the pan. Lightly oil the foil.

Put the sorghum flour, tapioca flour, teff flour, xanthan gum, and salt in a medium bowl. Stir with a dry whisk until combined.

Put the almond butter, agave nectar, and vanilla extract in the bowl of a stand mixer, with the paddle attachment, or a large bowl. Using the stand mixer or a hand mixer, beat until smooth, about 2 minutes. Add the flour mixture to the almond butter mixture. Beat on medium speed until the ingredients are well combined. The mixture will be thick.

Scrape the mixture into the lined pan using a rubber spatula. Press the mixture evenly into the pan using the spatula or your fingers. The consistency should be similar to that of cookie dough.

Bake for 12 to 14 minutes, just until the top is firm. Don't overbake. Let cool in the pan for about 30 minutes.

To make the topping, keep the oven at 350 degrees F. Put the almonds in a small bowl. Add the agave nectar, sugar, and salt. Mix well. Spread the mixture on an unlined baking sheet. Bake for about 8 minutes, stir the mixture, then bake for 7 minutes longer, until the mixture is bubbling and the almonds are fragrant. Put a piece of parchment paper or waxed paper on a flat surface. Scrape the mixture onto the parchment paper using a rubber spatula and spread it into a single layer. Let cool. The candied almonds will harden as they cool.

Per square (based on 25 squares): 206 calories, 5 g protein, 14 g fat (3 g sat), 15 g carbs, 56 mg sodium, 57 mg calcium, 3 g fiber

To make the filling, put the almond butter, agave nectar, coconut oil, and vanilla extract in the bowl of a stand mixer, with the paddle attachment, or a large bowl. Using the stand mixer or a hand mixer, beat until smooth and fluffy, about 2 minutes. Spread the filling over the base using the rubber spatula.

Once the candied almonds have hardened, chop them coarsely. Sprinkle them over the top of the filling, pressing down lightly so they stick. Refrigerate for 1 hour, until the filling is firm. (It won't harden completely.)

To cut and serve, use the foil to lift the contents out of the pan. Put the contents on a plate or in a container. Slice into squares using a sharp knife.

Stored in a sealed container, the squares will keep for 3 days in the refrigerator or 3 months in the freezer. If the house isn't too warm, they will keep in a sealed container for 3 days at room temperature.

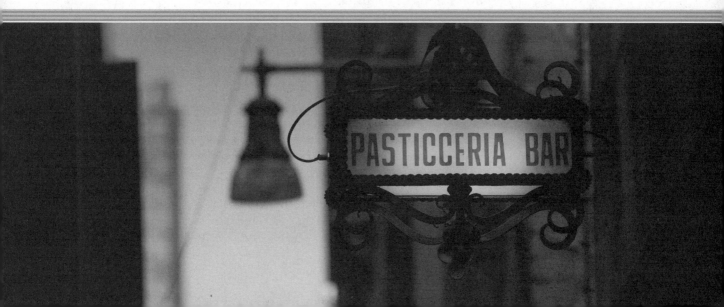

These morsels will remind you of **fresh bread** slathered with creamy peanut butter and mom's **homemade** strawberry jam. Bet you can't eat just one (pan).

Peanut Butter **AND JAM BLONDIES**

FREE OF: NUTS, SEEDS, YEAST   YIELD: 25 SMALL OR 16 MEDIUM BLONDIES

¾ cup unrefined cane sugar

¼ cup coconut oil, softened
(see page 18)

¾ cup creamy natural
peanut butter

2 teaspoons vanilla extract

¼ cup nondairy milk

2 tablespoons pure maple
syrup (grade A or B)

½ cup sorghum flour

¼ cup quinoa flour

¼ cup tapioca flour

¾ teaspoon xanthan gum

½ teaspoon baking powder

¼ teaspoon fine sea salt

¼ cup strawberry or
raspberry jam

Preheat the oven to 350 degrees F. Line an 8-inch square baking pan with aluminum foil, leaving a few inches of foil hanging over opposite sides of the pan. Lightly oil the foil.

Put the sugar and coconut oil in the bowl of a stand mixer, with the paddle attachment, or a large bowl. Using the stand mixer or a hand mixer, beat until smooth and well combined. Add the peanut butter and vanilla extract. Beat until well mixed, occasionally stopping to scrape down the bowl with a rubber spatula if necessary. Add the nondairy milk and maple syrup. Beat until combined.

Put the sorghum flour, quinoa flour, tapioca flour, xanthan gum, baking powder, and salt in a medium bowl. Stir with a dry whisk until combined.

Add the flour mixture to the peanut butter mixture. Beat on medium speed until well combined. The batter will be very thick.

Scrape the batter into the lined pan using a rubber spatula. Spread evenly to fill the pan. Put the handle of a fork or spoon in the batter (but don't scrape the bottom of the pan) and twist, creating small air pockets in the batter. Repeat 25 to 30 times throughout the batter. Spread the jam over the top of the batter using the rubber spatula. The air pockets will allow the jam to bake into the blondies rather than just sit on top.

Bake for 25 to 32 minutes, just until the edges are golden brown and the center is firm to the touch. Be careful not to overbake. Let cool completely in the pan.

Use the foil to lift the contents out of the pan. Put the contents on a plate or in a container. Slice into squares using a sharp knife.

Stored in a sealed container, the blondies will keep for 4 days at room temperature or in the refrigerator or 3 months in the freezer. The flavor will develop as the blondies sit, and they will be more flavorful the day after baking.

TIP: To avoid crumbly blondies, use well-mixed natural peanut butter, don't overbake the blondies, and let them cool in the pan. But if you happen to snag a few fresh out of the oven (and I know this from experience), they're still mighty good.

Per blondie (based on 25 blondies):
113 calories, 2 g protein, 6 g fat (3 g sat),
14 g carbs, 34 mg sodium, 8 mg calcium,
1 g fiber

Oh me, oh my. The winning **combination** of creamy chocolate, crunchy pecans, and tart raspberries will make these **mouthwatering** blondies a regular feature in your dessert rotation.

CHOCOLATE, PECAN, AND RASPBERRY *Blondies*

FREE OF: PEANUTS, YEAST   YIELD: 25 SMALL OR 16 MEDIUM BLONDIES

6 tablespoons vegan buttery spread, melted

1 tablespoon ground flaxseeds

¾ cup unrefined cane sugar

5 tablespoons nondairy milk (see tip)

1 teaspoon vanilla extract

½ cup sorghum flour

¼ cup quinoa flour

¼ cup tapioca flour

1 teaspoon fine sea salt

½ teaspoon xanthan gum

½ teaspoon baking powder

¾ cup pecans, toasted (see sidebar, page 13) **and chopped**

⅓ cup plus 3 tablespoons nondairy semisweet chocolate chips or chunks

¾ cup fresh raspberries, gently rinsed and well drained

Preheat the oven to 350 degrees F. Line an 8-inch square baking pan with aluminum foil, leaving a few inches of foil hanging over opposite sides of the pan. Lightly oil the foil.

Put the vegan buttery spread and flaxseeds in a medium bowl. Whisk well to combine. Add the sugar, nondairy milk, and vanilla extract. Mix well.

Put the sorghum flour, quinoa flour, tapioca flour, salt, xanthan gum, and baking powder in a medium bowl. Stir with a dry whisk until combined. Add the flour mixture to the sugar mixture. Mix until well combined. Stir in ½ cup of the pecans and ⅓ cup of the chocolate chips until evenly distributed.

Scrape the batter into the lined pan using a rubber spatula. Spread evenly. Smooth the top with the spatula. Sprinkle the remaining ¼ cup of pecans, the remaining 3 tablespoons of chocolate chips, and all of the raspberries on top of the batter. Press the pecans, chocolate chips, and raspberries lightly into the batter.

Bake for 35 to 45 minutes, until the edges are golden and a toothpick inserted in the center comes out clean. Be careful not to overbake. Let cool completely in the pan.

Use the foil to lift the contents out of the pan. Put the contents on a plate or in a container. Slice into squares using a sharp knife.

Stored in a sealed container, the blondies will keep for 3 days at room temperature or in the refrigerator or 3 months in the freezer.

TIP: For a richer blondie, replace the nondairy milk with full-fat canned coconut milk.

Per blondie (based on 25 blondies): 114 calories, 1 g protein, 7 g fat (2 g sat), 14 g carbs, 120 mg sodium, 20 mg calcium, 1 g fiber

These are the **best brownies you'll ever have,** but only if you like superfudgy, slightly nutty, melt-in-your-mouth brownies that are a little crispy on the edges and have just the right amount of crumb. If you *don't* like that kind of brownie, well, these aren't for you. But trust me, that's flat-out impossible.

Rich and Fudgy BROWNIES

FREE OF: LEGUMES, PEANUTS, YEAST   YIELD: 25 SMALL OR 16 MEDIUM BROWNIES

3 tablespoons warm water

1 tablespoon ground flaxseeds

¼ cup coconut oil, melted

¼ cup creamy roasted hazelnut butter

¼ cup brewed coffee or water, warm or cool (see tip, page 39)

1 cup unrefined cane sugar

½ cup unsweetened cocoa powder

2 tablespoons vanilla extract

½ cup teff flour

¼ cup sorghum flour

¼ cup arrowroot starch

¾ teaspoon xanthan gum

½ teaspoon baking powder

½ teaspoon fine sea salt

Preheat the oven to 325 degrees F. Line an 8-inch square baking pan with aluminum foil, leaving a few inches of foil hanging over opposite sides of the pan. Lightly oil the foil.

Put the water in a small bowl or measuring cup. Stir in the flaxseeds and let stand until thickened, about 5 minutes.

Put the coconut oil, hazelnut butter, and coffee in the bowl of a stand mixer, with the paddle attachment, or a large bowl. Using the stand mixer or a hand mixer, beat until smooth and well combined, about 2 minutes. Add the flaxseed mixture, sugar, cocoa powder, and vanilla extract. Beat until well mixed, occasionally stopping to scrape down the bowl with a rubber spatula if necessary.

Put the teff flour, sorghum flour, arrowroot starch, xanthan gum, baking powder, and salt in a medium bowl. Stir with a dry whisk until combined. Add the flour mixture to the hazelnut butter mixture. Beat on medium speed until well combined. The batter will be very thick.

Scrape the batter into the lined pan using a rubber spatula. Spread evenly, using lightly oiled hands if necessary. Smooth the top with the spatula.

Bake for 30 to 40 minutes, just until the top of the brownies is firm to the touch. Be careful not to overbake. Let cool completely in the pan. The flavor will further develop as the brownies cool.

Use the foil to lift the contents out of the pan. Put the contents on a plate or in a container. Slice into squares using a sharp knife.

Stored in a sealed container, the brownies will keep for 3 days at room temperature or in the refrigerator or 3 months in the freezer.

TIP: If you don't have hazelnut butter on hand, try using a different all-natural nut butter. Hazelnut butter delivers the best flavor, but other varieties will work in a pinch.

VARIATION: For extra chocolaty goodness, add ½ cup of chocolate chips or chocolate chunks to the batter before spreading it in the pan.

Per brownie (based on 25 brownies): 90 calories, 1 g protein, 4 g fat (2 g sat), 13 g carbs, 51 mg sodium, 15 mg calcium, 1 g fiber

These brownies are so **simple** to prepare, you don't even need an oven. I like to make them without the frosting and freeze them. That way, I have the perfect **on-the-go** or postworkout **snack** whenever I need it.

NO-BAKE FROSTED Mint Brownies

FREE OF: CORN, GRAINS, LEGUMES, PEANUTS, SEEDS, YEAST · YIELD: 12 BROWNIES

BROWNIES

1½ cups almonds

1 cup pitted soft honey dates (see page 11)

¼ cup raw cacao powder

¼ cup fresh mint or chocolate mint leaves, lightly packed

AVOCADO FROSTING

1 medium ripe avocado, flesh removed

¼ cup raw or light agave nectar

3 tablespoons raw cacao powder

To make the brownies, line an 8-inch square baking pan with parchment paper. Put the almonds in a food processor. Pulse until they are finely chopped, about 10 times. Add the dates, cacao powder, and mint. Process until the ingredients begin to stick together, about 3 minutes. The almonds should be finely ground and the dates smooth. To test, squeeze a small portion of the mixture in your hand. It should stick together. If it doesn't, pulse a few more times, being careful not to overprocess.

Scrape the mixture into the lined pan using a rubber spatula. Press the mixture evenly into the pan using the spatula.

To make the frosting, put the avocado flesh, agave nectar, and cacao powder in the food processor. Process until smooth. Scrape the frosting onto the brownies using a rubber spatula and spread evenly over the top of the brownies. Refrigerate for at least 4 hours before serving (see tip).

Stored in a sealed container, the brownies will keep for 5 days in the refrigerator, and unfrosted brownies will keep for 3 months in the freezer.

TIPS

- Because the mixture won't spread (since it isn't baked), you can use any size pan for this recipe, depending on how thick you prefer the brownies. For example, you can use an 8 x 4-inch loaf pan and press the mixture into it, but the brownies will be easier to remove and slice if you use a larger pan.

- Though the brownies can be enjoyed immediately after they are prepared, I recommend waiting for at least 4 hours so the brownies have time to become firm and the flavors have a chance to blend.

No-Bake Chocolate-Cherry Brownies: Omit the mint and stir in ½ cup of unsweetened dried cherries after processing the almonds, dates, and cacao powder in the food processor.

Per brownie: 200 calories, 5 g protein, 11 g fat (1 g sat), 22 g carbs, 2 mg sodium, 61 mg calcium, 5 g fiber

If I had to choose a *favorite recipe* in this book, this might be it. After all, what could be better than the marriage of these two classics? I can only think of one thing: topping this dessert with Chocolate-Macadamia Frosting (page 64) and calling it my *birthday cake*.

BROWNIES TOPPED WITH Chocolate Chip Cookie Dough

FREE OF: LEGUMES, NUTS, PEANUTS, SEEDS, YEAST   YIELD: 25 SMALL OR 16 MEDIUM BROWNIES

BROWNIES

½ cup unsweetened cocoa powder, sifted

½ cup teff flour

¼ cup sorghum flour

¼ cup tapioca flour

¾ teaspoon xanthan gum

½ teaspoon baking powder

½ teaspoon fine sea salt

¾ cup unrefined cane sugar

6 tablespoons unsweetened applesauce

6 tablespoons coconut oil, softened or melted (see page 18)

¼ cup nondairy milk

2 teaspoons vanilla extract

To make the brownies, preheat the oven to 350 degrees F. Line an 8-inch square baking pan with aluminum foil, leaving a few inches of foil hanging over opposite sides of the pan. Lightly oil the foil.

Put the cocoa powder, teff flour, sorghum flour, tapioca flour, xanthan gum, baking powder, and salt in a medium bowl. Stir with a dry whisk until combined.

Put the sugar, applesauce, coconut oil, nondairy milk, and vanilla extract in the bowl of a stand mixer, with the paddle attachment, or a large bowl. Using the stand mixer or a hand mixer, beat until smooth and well combined, about 2 minutes. The mixture might look curdled—don't worry, this is normal. Add the flour mixture. Beat until well mixed, occasionally stopping to scrape down the bowl with a rubber spatula if necessary.

Scrape the batter into the lined pan using a rubber spatula, spreading it evenly. Smooth the top with the spatula. Bake for 20 minutes. Remove from the oven but keep the oven on.

Per brownie (based on 25 brownies): 175 calories, 2 g protein, 10 g fat (8 g sat), 23 g carbs, 94 mg sodium, 21 mg calcium, 2 g fiber

CHOCOLATE CHIP COOKIE DOUGH

1/2 cup unrefined cane sugar

1/2 cup coconut oil, softened
(see page 18)

1 1/2 tablespoons nondairy milk

2 teaspoons vanilla extract

3/4 cup sorghum flour

6 tablespoons tapioca flour

1/2 teaspoon xanthan gum

1/4 teaspoon plus 1/8 teaspoon
baking soda

1/4 teaspoon fine sea salt

1/2 cup nondairy semisweet
chocolate chips

To make the cookie dough, put the sugar and coconut oil in the bowl of a stand mixer or a large bowl. Using the stand mixer or a hand mixer, beat until smooth and creamy, about 2 minutes. Add the nondairy milk and vanilla extract. Beat until combined.

Put the sorghum flour, tapioca flour, xanthan gum, baking soda, and salt in a medium bowl. Stir with a dry whisk until combined. Turn the mixer to low speed. Add the flour mixture to the sugar mixture. Beat until combined. Turn off the mixer. Stir in the chocolate chips until evenly distributed.

Drop the cookie dough in rounded teaspoonfuls evenly over the top of the partially baked brownies, pressing it down very lightly. Bake for 8 to 12 minutes, until a toothpick inserted in the center of the brownies comes out clean and the chocolate chip cookie topping has started to turn golden. Do not over-bake. Let cool for at least 15 minutes in the pan. The flavor will further develop as the contents cool.

To cut and serve, use the foil to lift the contents out of the pan. Put the contents on a plate or in a container. Let cool completely. Slice into squares using a sharp knife.

Stored in a sealed container, the brownies will keep for 4 days at room temperature or 3 months in the freezer.

Inspired by the popular triple-layer British bar cookie, this version has a base of buttery shortbread topped with creamy caramel and smooth chocolate. The taste is so heavenly, you'll think you've struck it rich.

Billionaire's SHORTBREAD

FREE OF: LEGUMES,* PEANUTS, SEEDS, YEAST   YIELD: 20 BARS

SHORTBREAD BASE

¾ cup sorghum flour

½ cup cornstarch

¼ cup quinoa flour

Heaping ¼ cup confectioners' sugar, sifted

¾ teaspoon xanthan gum

¼ teaspoon fine sea salt

½ cup coconut oil, softened or melted (see page 18) ·

½ teaspoon vanilla extract

CREAMY CARAMEL FILLING

1 cup creamy roasted or raw cashew butter

3 tablespoons pure maple syrup (grade A or B)

3 tablespoons light agave nectar

2 tablespoons water, plus more as needed

½ teaspoon blackstrap molasses

¼ teaspoon fine sea salt

2 teaspoons arrowroot starch or sweet rice flour

To make the base, preheat the oven to 350 degrees F. Line a 9-inch square baking pan with parchment paper, leaving a few inches of paper hanging over opposite sides of the pan.

Put the sorghum flour, cornstarch, quinoa flour, confectioners' sugar, xanthan gum, and salt in the bowl of a stand mixer, with the paddle attachment, or a large bowl. Stir with a dry whisk until combined. Turn the stand mixer or a hand mixer to low speed. Add the coconut oil and vanilla extract. Turn the mixer to medium speed. Beat until combined. The mixture should hold together when you squeeze a portion of it in your hand.

Scrape the mixture into the lined pan using a rubber spatula. Press the mixture evenly into the pan using the spatula or your fingers. Bake for 18 to 20 minutes, until the top is firm and the edges begin to pull away from the sides of the pan. Don't overbake or the base will become crumbly. Put the pan on a cooling rack to cool for at least 20 minutes.

To make the filling, put the cashew butter, maple syrup, agave nectar, water, molasses, and salt in a small saucepan. Bring to a simmer over medium heat. Cook just until the mixture begins to bubble, about 2 minutes. Stir in the arrowroot starch and cook for 1 minute longer. The filling should be creamy, thick, and smooth. If it's too thick to stir, or if it's dry and separates, stir in up to 2 tablespoons additional water, 1 teaspoon at a time.

Scrape the filling onto the slightly cooled base using a rubber spatula and carefully spread the filling evenly over the top of the base. Put the pan in the freezer for 20 minutes.

Per bar: 235 calories, 3 g protein, 16 g fat (9 g sat), 22 g carbs, 68 mg sodium, 21 mg calcium, 2 g fiber

CHOCOLATE TOPPING

¾ cup nondairy semisweet chocolate chips

2 tablespoons vegan buttery spread
(*use coconut oil for legume-free)

To make the topping, put the chocolate chips and vegan buttery spread in a microwave-safe bowl. Microwave on high for 15 seconds and stir. Repeat as needed until the chocolate has melted and the mixture is smooth. To melt the chocolate on the stovetop, fill a small saucepan with one inch of water. Bring to a simmer over medium heat. Put a glass bowl on top of the saucepan, making sure it doesn't touch the water but creates a seal to trap the steam produced by the simmering water. Put the chocolate chips and vegan buttery spread in the bowl. As the bowl heats, the chocolate will begin to melt. Stir occasionally, until the chocolate is completely melted.

Remove the pan from the freezer. Spread the topping evenly over the filling using a metal offset spatula. Score the top into 20 bars using a sharp knife. This will make it easier to cut the bars and prevent the topping from cracking. Refrigerate until the topping has hardened and the filling is set, at least 3 hours.

To cut and serve, use the parchment paper to lift the contents out of the pan. Put the contents on a plate or in a container. Dip a sharp knife into very hot water before slicing into bars to prevent the topping from cracking.

Stored in a sealed container, the bars will keep for 3 days in the refrigerator or 3 months in the freezer.

My favorite time to make these satisfying squares *is when local apples are at their peak. The house* smells wonderful *while they are baking.*

Apple Crumb SQUARES

FREE OF: NUTS, PEANUTS, SEEDS, YEAST

YIELD: 25 SMALL OR 16 MEDIUM SQUARES

BASE AND CRUMBLE TOPPING

1 cup sorghum flour

1/2 cup unrefined cane sugar

1/4 cup quinoa flour

1/4 cup tapioca flour

2 teaspoons ground flaxseeds

1 1/2 teaspoons xanthan gum

1/2 teaspoon baking powder

1/4 teaspoon fine sea salt

1/2 cup vegan buttery spread

1 1/2 tablespoons nondairy milk, plus more as needed

1/2 teaspoon vanilla extract

APPLE FILLING

4 cups grated sweet baking apples, such as Gala (about 4 apples)

1 1/2 tablespoons freshly squeezed lemon juice

3 1/2 tablespoons cornstarch

2 teaspoons ground cinnamon

1/2 teaspoon ground nutmeg

1/4 teaspoon fine sea salt

1/4 cup unrefined cane sugar

To make the base and crumble topping, preheat the oven to 375 degrees F. Lightly oil an 8-inch square baking pan.

Put the sorghum flour, sugar, quinoa flour, tapioca flour, flaxseeds, xanthan gum, baking powder, and salt in a large bowl. Stir with a dry whisk until combined. Add the vegan buttery spread, nondairy milk, and vanilla extract. Use a pastry blender or two knives to cut the mixture until it resembles moist, coarse crumbs. To test, squeeze a small portion of the mixture in your hand. It should stick together. If it doesn't, add additional nondairy milk, about 1 teaspoon at a time, until the desired consistency is achieved. Press half of the mixture evenly into the prepared pan using the back of a fork or your fingers. Reserve the other half for the crumble topping.

To make the filling, put the apples in a medium bowl. Add the lemon juice and toss until the apples are coated. Transfer the apple mixture to a sieve and let drain over a bowl, until you have 1/3 cup of liquid for the glaze (squeeze the apples if necessary). If you have more than 1/3 cup of liquid, return the apple mixture to the bowl and stir in the excess liquid. Add the cornstarch, cinnamon, nutmeg, and salt to the apple mixture. Mix well, until no traces of cornstarch are visible. Add the sugar and mix well. Scrape the filling onto the base using a rubber spatula and spread evenly over the top of the base.

Use the reserved base mixture to make the crumble topping by forming the mixture into small clumps using your fingers. Sprinkle the clumps on top of the filling, pressing down lightly.

Bake for 45 to 55 minutes, until the apples are cooked through and the topping is golden brown. Check for doneness after 35 minutes. If the topping appears to be overbrowning, tent with aluminum foil. Let cool completely in the pan.

Per square (based on 25 squares): 106 calories, 1 g protein, 4 g fat (1 g sat), 18 g carbs, 94 mg sodium, 10 mg calcium, 1 g fiber

APPLE GLAZE

⅓ cup liquid from draining the grated apples

⅓ cup confectioners' sugar, sifted

¼ teaspoon vanilla extract

⅛ teaspoon fine sea salt

Nondairy milk, as needed

To make the glaze, put the drained liquid from the apple mixture in a small saucepan. Bring to a boil over high heat and cook until the liquid is reduced to about 2 tablespoons. Put the confectioners' sugar in a small bowl. Add the reduced liquid, vanilla extract, and salt. Mix until smooth. The mixture should be thick but still run off a spoon. If the mixture is too thick, stir in the nondairy milk, ½ teaspoon at a time, as needed to achieve the desired consistency. Spoon the glaze over the crumble topping. Refrigerate until the glaze is firm, about 15 minutes.

To cut and serve, slice into squares using a sharp knife. Serve at room temperature or cold.

Stored in a sealed container, the squares will keep for 3 days in the refrigerator.

TIPS

- Use a box grater, not a food processor, to grate the apples. Apples grated in a food processor release excess moisture, which will make these squares soggy. Before grating, cut each unpeeled apple into four sections. Cut out and discard the core.

- Don't add the sugar to the apple filling until just before you put it in the pan. Otherwise, the apples will start to break down and release too much liquid.

If you are a pumpkin pie fan, you'll love these treats, which have a buttery pecan base, a creamy pumpkin filling, and a crunchy pecan topping. What if you don't like pumpkin pie? Chances are *you'll devour these* anyway, especially if they're served alongside a steaming mug of apple cider.

Pumpkin Pie SQUARES WITH PECAN CRUMBLE

FREE OF: PEANUTS, SEEDS, YEAST   YIELD: 25 SMALL OR 16 MEDIUM SQUARES

PECAN SHORTBREAD BASE

⅔ cup pecans, toasted (see sidebar, page 13)

½ cup sorghum flour

⅓ cup unrefined cane sugar

¼ cup teff flour

¼ cup arrowroot starch

¾ teaspoon xanthan gum

6 tablespoons vegan buttery spread

PUMPKIN FILLING

2 cups mashed cooked or canned pumpkin (not pie filling)

⅓ cup unrefined cane sugar

⅓ cup pure maple syrup (grade A or B)

¼ cup nondairy milk

3 tablespoons sorghum flour

2 tablespoons arrowroot starch

2 teaspoons ground cinnamon

1 teaspoon vanilla extract

½ teaspoon ground ginger

½ teaspoon ground nutmeg

⅛ teaspoon ground cloves

⅛ teaspoon fine sea salt

To make the base, preheat the oven to 350 degrees F. Line an 8-inch square baking pan with aluminum foil, leaving a few inches of foil hanging over opposite sides of the pan. Lightly oil the foil.

Put the pecans, sorghum flour, sugar, teff flour, arrowroot starch, and xanthan gum in a food processor. Process until the pecans are finely chopped. Add the vegan buttery spread. Process just until the mixture starts to come together in a cohesive ball. Turn off the food processor.

Scrape the mixture into the lined pan using a rubber spatula. Press the mixture evenly into the pan using the spatula. Prick with a fork in about six places. Bake for 20 minutes until firm to the touch but not baked through. Remove from the oven but keep the oven on.

To make the filling, put the pumpkin, sugar, maple syrup, nondairy milk, sorghum flour, arrowroot starch, cinnamon, vanilla extract, ginger, nutmeg, cloves, and salt in the food processor. Process until smooth. Scrape the filling onto the base using the rubber spatula and spread evenly over the top of the base.

Per square (based on 25 squares): 112 calories, 1 g protein, 6 g fat (1 g sat), 14 g carbs, 37 mg sodium, 15 mg calcium, 2 g fiber

PECAN CRUMBLE TOPPING

⅓ **cup pecans, toasted** (see sidebar, page 13) **and finely chopped**

2 tablespoons sorghum flour

1 tablespoon unrefined cane sugar

1 tablespoon vegan buttery spread, melted

To make the topping, put the pecans, sorghum flour, and sugar in a small bowl. Mix in the vegan buttery spread until the pecans are well coated. Sprinkle the topping evenly over the filling.

Bake for 40 to 50 minutes, until the edges and top are firm. Let cool in the pan for 10 minutes.

To cut and serve, use the foil to lift the contents out of the pan. Put the contents on a cooling rack to cool completely before slicing (if you find this difficult, let the contents cool longer in the pan). Serve at room temperature or cold. The flavor will deepen as the bars cool; they will taste more flavorful the day after baking.

Stored in a sealed container, the squares will keep for 4 days in the refrigerator.

TIPS

- If you prefer spicier pumpkin desserts, sample the filling before you scrape it onto the base. If desired, add 1 teaspoon additional ground cinnamon, 1 teaspoon additional ground ginger, ¼ teaspoon additional ground nutmeg, and ⅛ teaspoon additional ground cloves.

- You can also bake this in a 9-inch round pan and serve it pie-style. For an elegant fall dinner-party dessert, top a slice with a scoop of vanilla coconut milk ice cream and a dusting of cinnamon sugar.

In this **twist on the classic** date square, chopped pear partners perfectly with soft dates and buckwheat cereal adds texture. These star ingredients are complemented by a **hint of orange** flavor and just the right amount of **sweetness.**

GLAZED Date and Pear SQUARES

FREE OF: NUTS, PEANUTS, SEEDS, YEAST   YIELD: 25 SMALL OR 16 MEDIUM SQUARES

DATE AND PEAR FILLING

1 cup pitted soft honey dates (see page 11)

1 ripe pear, cored and chopped into ¼-inch pieces (peel before coring if desired)

2 teaspoons finely grated orange zest (about ½ orange)

1 teaspoon ground cinnamon

6 tablespoons freshly squeezed orange juice

2 teaspoons cornstarch

BUCKWHEAT BASE AND CRUMBLE TOPPING

½ cup creamy buckwheat cereal, uncooked (see page 15)

½ cup unrefined cane sugar

½ cup sorghum flour

¼ cup quinoa flour

¼ cup arrowroot starch

1 tablespoon ground flaxseeds

1 teaspoon xanthan gum

½ teaspoon baking powder

⅛ teaspoon fine sea salt

½ cup vegan buttery spread

1 tablespoon nondairy milk

To make the filling, put the dates, pear, orange zest, and cinnamon in a medium saucepan. Put the orange juice and cornstarch in a measuring cup or small bowl. Whisk until smooth. Add the orange juice mixture to the date mixture and stir until combined. Bring to a boil over medium-high heat. Decrease the heat to medium-low and cook, stirring often, until the mixture becomes thick and the dates are soft, 2 to 3 minutes. Remove from the heat. Mash the dates with a fork. (Some pieces of pear should remain intact.) Stir until well combined. Let cool while you prepare the base.

To make the base and crumble topping, preheat the oven to 375 degrees F. Lightly oil an 8-inch square pan.

Put the buckwheat cereal, sugar, sorghum flour, quinoa flour, arrowroot starch, flaxseeds, xanthan gum, baking powder, and salt in a small bowl. Stir with a dry whisk until combined. Add the vegan buttery spread and nondairy milk. Use a pastry blender or two knives to cut the mixture until it resembles moist, coarse crumbs. The mixture should stick together when you squeeze a portion of it in your hand. Remove a heaping ½ cup of the mixture to reserve for the crumble topping. Press the remaining mixture evenly into the pan using the back of a fork or your fingers. Bake for 15 to 18 minutes, just until the top is firm to the touch. Remove from the oven but keep the oven on.

Scrape the filling onto the base using the rubber spatula and spread evenly over the top of the base. Use the reserved base mixture to make the crumble topping by forming the mixture into small clumps using your fingers. Sprinkle the clumps on top of the filling, pressing down lightly. Bake for 24 to 30 minutes, until golden brown. Let cool completely in the pan.

Per square (based on 25 squares): 115 calories, 1 g protein, 4 g fat (1 g sat), 19 g carbs, 52 mg sodium, 14 mg calcium, 2 g fiber

ORANGE DRIZZLE

½ cup confectioners' sugar, sifted

1 tablespoon freshly squeezed orange juice

To make the drizzle, put the confectioners' sugar in a small bowl. Add the orange juice. Mix until smooth. Spoon the drizzle over the crumble topping. Refrigerate until the drizzle is firm, about 15 minutes.

To cut and serve, slice into squares using a sharp knife. Serve at room temperature or cold.

Stored in a sealed container in the refrigerator, the squares will keep for 3 days.

These **versatile bars** are a blank canvas, just waiting for your personal touch. **Go ahead,** experiment, and make these no-bake bars your own.

NUTTY AND CRUNCHY No-Bake Bars

FREE OF: CORN, LEGUMES, PEANUTS, YEAST   YIELD: 18 BARS

½ cup chopped almonds

½ cup chopped walnuts or pecans

¼ cup ground flaxseeds

¼ cup unsweetened finely shredded dried coconut

3 tablespoons hempseeds

1½ cups gluten-free crispy brown rice cereal (see page 15)

¾ cup gluten-free puffed quinoa cereal

½ cup raisins or dried cranberries

½ cup light agave nectar

¼ cup creamy roasted almond butter

1½ teaspoons ground cinnamon

½ teaspoon fine sea salt

1 teaspoon vanilla extract

Line a 9-inch square baking pan with aluminum foil, leaving a few inches of foil hanging over opposite sides of the pan. Lightly oil the foil.

Put the almonds, walnuts, flaxseeds, coconut, and hempseeds in a large skillet over medium heat. Cook for 5 minutes, stirring frequently, until fragrant and toasted. Immediately transfer to a large bowl to cool. (The almond mixture will burn if left to cool in the skillet.)

Once the almond mixture has cooled, add the rice cereal, quinoa cereal, and raisins. Mix well.

Put the agave nectar, almond butter, cinnamon, and salt in a small saucepan. Stir to combine. Bring to a simmer over medium heat. Cook, stirring constantly, until the mixture resembles a thick syrup, about 4 minutes. Remove from the heat. Stir in the vanilla extract.

Add the almond butter mixture to the cereal mixture. Mix well to combine. Scrape the mixture into the lined pan using a rubber spatula. Press the mixture evenly into the pan using the back of a fork. Refrigerate until hardened, at least 30 minutes. For the best results, refrigerate for 4 hours or longer before serving.

Use the foil to lift the contents out of the pan. Slice into bars or squares using a sharp knife. Wrap individually in plastic wrap.

Stored in a sealed container, the bars will keep for 1 week in the refrigerator or 3 months in the freezer.

TIP: Feel free to substitute your favorites for the nuts, seeds, cereals, dried fruit, and nut butter. Or try maple syrup instead of agave nectar, add cacao nibs or chocolate chips, or replace the quinoa puffs with amaranth puffs.

Per bar: 149 calories, 3 g protein, 9 g fat (1 g sat), 17 g carbs, 79 mg sodium, 32 mg calcium, 2 g fiber

These crisp, slightly tender biscotti have just the right amount of nutty almond crunch. Don't worry if you don't like banana—you won't even taste it, since chocolate is the dominant flavor.

CHOCOLATE-ALMOND Biscotti

FREE OF: PEANUTS, YEAST   YIELD: 24 BISCOTTI

3 tablespoons warm water

1 tablespoon ground flaxseeds

¼ cup vegan buttery spread

Scant 1 cup unrefined cane sugar

¼ cup mashed banana
   (1 small banana)

1 teaspoon vanilla extract

1 cup sorghum flour

½ cup teff flour

½ cup arrowroot starch

½ cup unsweetened cocoa powder, sifted

1½ teaspoons xanthan gum

1 teaspoon baking powder

½ teaspoon baking soda

½ teaspoon fine sea salt

1 cup almonds, toasted
   (see sidebar, page 13)

¾ cup nondairy semisweet chocolate chips

Preheat the oven to 350 degrees F. Line a baking sheet with parchment paper.

Put the water in a small bowl or measuring cup. Stir in the flaxseeds and let stand until thickened, about 5 minutes.

Put the vegan buttery spread in the bowl of a stand mixer, with the paddle attachment, or a large bowl. Using the stand mixer or a hand mixer, beat until smooth, about 2 minutes. Add the sugar. Beat for an additional 2 minutes. Add the banana, vanilla extract, and flaxseed mixture. Beat until all ingredients are well combined.

Put the sorghum flour, teff flour, arrowroot starch, cocoa powder, xanthan gum, baking powder, baking soda, and salt in a medium bowl. Stir with a dry whisk until combined. Turn the mixer to low speed. Gradually add the flour mixture to the sugar mixture, beating until just mixed. The dough will be very stiff. Using a spoon, or your hands if necessary, mix in the almonds and chocolate chips until evenly distributed.

Using lightly floured hands, transfer the dough to the lined baking sheet. Form into two logs, each about 8 x 3 inches. Bake for 25 to 30 minutes, or until firm to the touch but not hard. Let cool on the baking sheet for at least 10 minutes.

Decrease the oven temperature to 300 degrees F. Carefully transfer the logs to a cutting board. Cut each log into ¾-inch slices on the diagonal using a sharp chef's knife. Cut in one fluid motion; do not saw. Remove the parchment paper from the baking sheet. Put the slices bottom-side down on the baking sheet. Bake for 15 minutes. Turn the slices onto one side. Bake for 5 to 10 minutes, until toasted. Carefully turn the slices over and continue baking for 5 to 10 minutes, until crisp. Transfer to a cooling rack to cool completely. The biscotti will continue to firm after they have cooled.

Stored in a sealed container, the biscotti will keep for 1 week at room temperature or 3 months in the freezer.

Per biscotti: 164 calories, 3 g protein, 8 g fat (2 g sat), 23 g carbs, 102 mg sodium, 39 mg calcium, 3 g fiber

Laced with **maple and cinnamon,** this glazed biscotti has **extra crunch** thanks to the addition of buckwheat cereal. Serve alongside a cold glass of nondairy milk or a mug of steaming coffee or tea for dunking.

Maple-Cinnamon BISCOTTI

FREE OF: LEGUMES, NUTS, PEANUTS, SEEDS, YEAST   YIELD: 24 BISCOTTI

MAPLE-CINNAMON BISCOTTI

3 tablespoons warm water

1 tablespoon ground flaxseeds

1 cup sorghum flour

¾ cup creamy buckwheat cereal, uncooked (see page 15)

½ cup quinoa flour

½ cup arrowroot starch

2 teaspoons ground cinnamon

1½ teaspoons xanthan gum

1 teaspoon baking powder

½ teaspoon baking soda

½ teaspoon ground nutmeg

½ teaspoon fine sea salt

½ cup pure maple syrup (preferably grade B)

½ cup unrefined cane sugar

1 tablespoon canola oil or coconut oil, melted

1 teaspoon vanilla extract

To make the biscotti, preheat the oven to 350 degrees F. Line a baking sheet with parchment paper.

Put the water in the bowl of a stand mixer, with the paddle attachment, or a large bowl. Stir in the flaxseeds and let stand until thickened, about 5 minutes.

Put the sorghum flour, buckwheat cereal, quinoa flour, arrowroot starch, cinnamon, xanthan gum, baking powder, baking soda, nutmeg, and salt in a medium bowl. Stir with a dry whisk until combined.

Add the maple syrup, sugar, oil, and vanilla extract to the flaxseed mixture. Using the stand mixer or a hand mixer, beat until smooth, about 2 minutes. Turn the mixer to low speed. Gradually add the flour mixture to the sugar mixture, beating until just mixed. The dough will be stiff.

Using lightly floured hands, transfer the dough to the lined baking sheet. Form into two logs, each about 8 x 3 inches. Bake for 25 to 30 minutes, until firm to the touch but not hard. Let cool on the baking sheet for at least 10 minutes.

Decrease the oven temperature to 300 degrees F. Carefully transfer the logs to a cutting board. Cut each log into ¾-inch slices on the diagonal using a sharp chef's knife. Cut in one fluid motion; do not saw. Put the slices cut-side down on the lined baking sheet. Bake for 15 minutes, until toasted. Carefully turn the slices over and continue baking for 5 to 10 minutes, until crisp. Transfer to a cooling rack to cool completely. The biscotti will continue to firm after they have cooled.

Per biscotti: 107 calories, 2 g protein, 1 g fat (0.1 g sat), 23 g carbs, 90 mg sodium, 16 mg calcium, 1 g fiber

MAPLE GLAZE

½ cup confectioners' sugar, sifted

1 teaspoon maple extract

1 teaspoon nondairy milk, plus more as needed

To make the glaze, put the confectioners' sugar in a small bowl. Add the maple extract and nondairy milk. Mix until smooth. The mixture should be thin enough to drizzle but still thick. Add just enough additional nondairy milk to achieve the desired consistency.

Put a sheet of parchment paper or waxed paper on a flat surface. Put the biscotti cut-side down on the parchment paper. Dip a fork in the glaze and quickly drizzle it over the biscotti using a back-and-forth motion. Let the glaze set completely before serving or storing.

Stored in a sealed container, the biscotti will keep for 1 week at room temperature or 3 months in the freezer.

Who can resist the **combination** of caramel, pecans, and chocolate? Cashew butter makes this biscotti crisp on the outside and a little tender on the inside, while the dates deliver bursts of caramel-like sweetness throughout. Crunchy pecans and a chocolate drizzle add **fantastic flavor and texture.**

CASHEW BUTTER-DATE Biscotti

FREE OF: PEANUTS, SEEDS, YEAST   YIELD: 26 BISCOTTI

BISCOTTI

1 cup sorghum flour

½ cup quinoa flour

½ cup arrowroot starch

1½ teaspoons xanthan gum

1½ teaspoons baking powder

¼ teaspoon fine sea salt

⅔ cup unrefined cane sugar

¼ cup vegan buttery spread

½ cup creamy roasted cashew
   butter

½ cup unsweetened applesauce

1 teaspoon vanilla extract

¾ cup pitted soft honey dates
   (see page 11)

¾ cup pecans, toasted (see
   sidebar, page 13)

CHOCOLATE DRIZZLE

¼ cup nondairy semisweet
   chocolate chips

To make the biscotti, preheat the oven to 350 degrees F. Line a baking sheet with parchment paper.

Put the sorghum flour, quinoa flour, arrowroot starch, xanthan gum, baking powder, and salt in a medium bowl. Stir with a dry whisk until combined.

Put the sugar and vegan buttery spread in the bowl of a stand mixer, with the paddle attachment, or a large bowl. Using the stand mixer or a hand mixer, beat until smooth, about 2 minutes. Add the cashew butter, applesauce, and vanilla extract. Beat until smooth and very creamy.

Turn the mixer to low speed. Gradually add the flour mixture to the cashew butter mixture, beating until just mixed. The dough will be stiff. Using a spoon, or your hands if necessary, mix in the dates and pecans until evenly distributed.

Using lightly floured hands, transfer the dough to the lined baking sheet. Form into two logs, each about 8 x 3 inches. Bake for 25 to 30 minutes, until firm to the touch but not hard. Let cool on the baking sheet for at least 10 minutes.

Decrease the oven temperature to 300 degrees F. Carefully transfer the logs to a cutting board. Cut each log into ¾-inch slices on the diagonal using a sharp chef's knife. Cut using one fluid motion; do not saw. Remove the parchment paper from the baking sheet. Put the slices bottom-side down on the baking sheet. Bake for 15 minutes. Turn the slices onto one side. Bake for 5 to 10 minutes, until toasted. Carefully turn the slices over and bake for 5 to 10 minutes, until firm. Transfer to a cooling rack to cool completely. The biscotti will continue to firm after they have cooled.

Per biscotti: 146 calories, 2 g protein, 7 g fat (2 g sat), 20 g carbs, 54 mg sodium, 22 mg calcium, 2 g fiber

To make the drizzle, put the chocolate chips in a microwave-safe bowl. Microwave on high for 15 seconds and stir. Repeat as needed until the chocolate is melted and smooth. To melt the chocolate on the stovetop, fill a small saucepan with one inch of water. Bring to a simmer over medium heat. Put a glass bowl on top of the saucepan, making sure it doesn't touch the water but creates a seal to trap the steam produced by the simmering water. Put the chocolate chips in the bowl. As the bowl heats, the chocolate will begin to melt. Stir occasionally, until the chocolate is completely melted.

Put a sheet of parchment paper or waxed paper on a flat surface. Put the biscotti cut-side down on the parchment paper. Dip a fork in the melted chocolate and quickly drizzle it over the biscotti in a back-and-forth motion. Let harden completely before serving or storing.

Stored in a sealed container, the biscotti will keep for 1 week at room temperature or 3 months in the freezer.

This **low-fat** biscotti recipe features toasted hazelnuts. Use this as a **basic recipe** to make your own variation by using other types of nuts or replacing the hazelnuts with dried fruit or chocolate chips.

HAZELNUT Biscotti

FREE OF: LEGUMES, PEANUTS, SEEDS, YEAST   YIELD: 18 BISCOTTI

½ cup sorghum flour

½ cup teff flour

½ cup arrowroot starch

1 teaspoon baking powder

1 teaspoon xanthan gum

¼ teaspoon fine sea salt

¾ cup unrefined cane sugar

6 tablespoons applesauce

1½ tablespoons canola oil

1 teaspoon vanilla extract

1 teaspoon hazelnut extract (see tip)

¾ cup hazelnuts, toasted (see sidebar, page 13) **and chopped**

Preheat the oven to 325 degrees F. Line a baking sheet with parchment paper.

Put the sorghum flour, teff flour, arrowroot starch, baking powder, xanthan gum, and salt in a small bowl. Stir with a dry whisk until combined.

Put the sugar, applesauce, oil, vanilla extract, and hazelnut extract in the bowl of a stand mixer, with the paddle attachment, or a large bowl. Using the stand mixer or a hand mixer, beat until smooth, about 2 minutes. Turn the mixer to low speed. Gradually add the flour mixture to the sugar mixture, beating until just mixed. The dough will be stiff. Using a spoon, or your hands if necessary, mix in the hazelnuts until evenly distributed.

Using lightly floured hands, transfer the dough to the lined baking sheet. Form into two logs, each about 6 x 3 inches. Bake for 25 to 30 minutes, until firm to the touch but not hard. Let cool on the baking sheet for at least 10 minutes.

Decrease the oven temperature to 300 degrees F. Cut each log into ¾-inch slices on the diagonal using a sharp chef's knife. Cut in one fluid motion; do not saw. Remove the parchment paper from the baking sheet. Put the slices bottom-side down on the baking sheet. Bake for 10 minutes. Turn the slices onto one side and bake for 5 to 10 minutes, until toasted. Carefully turn the slices over and bake for 5 to 10 minutes, until firm. Transfer to a cooling rack to cool completely. The biscotti will continue to firm after they have cooled.

Stored in a sealed container, the biscotti will keep for 1 week at room temperature or 3 months in the freezer.

TIP: If you don't have hazelnut extract on hand, add 1½ teaspoons additional vanilla extract.

Per biscotti: 118 calories, 2 g protein, 5 g fat (0.3 g sat), 18 g carbs, 47 mg sodium, 21 mg calcium, 2 g fiber

PART IV

The Extras

CONVERSIONS

T he following tables provide information to help you make conversions if necessary. This book uses conventional measures; conventional pan sizes are listed in table 10, page 138. Metric equivalents can be found in table 11, page 139. Before substituting pan sizes and shapes, keep these points in mind:

- To measure the depth of a pan, measure the middle of the pan.
- To measure the length and width of a pan, measure from the inside edges.
- To measure the volume of a pan, use a measuring cup to fill the pan to the brim with water. The volume of the pan is equal to the amount of water required to fill it.
- When using dark baking pans or glass baking dishes instead of light-colored metal pans, decrease the oven temperature by 25 degrees F.
- Food will bake more quickly in a larger pan, so decrease the baking time accordingly.

PAN	CAPACITY	SUBSTITUTIONS	
1 (8-inch) round pan	4 cups	1 (8 x 4-inch) loaf pan 1 (9-inch) pie plate	1 (9-inch) round pan
1 (8 x 4-inch) loaf pan	6 cups	1 (8-inch) round pan	1 (11 x 7-inch) baking dish
1 (9-inch) round pan	6 cups	1 (8-inch) round pan 1 (8 x 4-inch) loaf pan	1 (11 x 7-inch) baking dish
1 (11 x 7 x 2-inch) baking dish	6 cups	1 (8-inch) square baking dish 1 (9-inch) round pan	1 (9-inch) square baking dish
1 (8-inch square) baking dish	8 cups	1 (9 x 2-inch) deep-dish pie plate 1 (9 x 5-inch) loaf pan	2 (8-inch) pie plates
1 (9-inch square) baking dish	8 cups	1 (9 x 2-inch) deep-dish pie plate 1 (9 x 5-inch) loaf pan	1 (11 x 7-inch) baking dish 2 (8-inch) pie plates
1 (9 x 5-inch) loaf pan	8 cups	1 (8-inch) square baking dish 1 (9-inch) square baking dish	1 (9 x 2-inch) deep-dish pie plate 1 (10-inch) pie plate
2 (8-inch) round pans	8 cups	1 (9-inch) tube pan 1 (10-inch) Bundt pan 1 (10-inch) springform pan	1 (11 x 7-inch) baking dish 2 (8 x 4-inch) loaf pans 2 (9-inch) round pans
1 (9-inch) springform pan	10 cups	1 (10-inch) round pan 1 (10-inch) springform pan	2 (8-inch) round pans 2 (9-inch) round pans
1 (10-inch) round pan	11 cups	1 (9-inch) tube pan 1 (10-inch) springform pan	2 (8-inch) round pans
1 (9-inch) tube pan	12 cups	1 (10-inch) Bundt pan 2 (8-inch) round pans	2 (9-inch) round pans
1 (10-inch) Bundt pan	12 cups	1 (9-inch) tube pan 1 (13 x 9-inch) baking dish 1 (10-inch) springform pan	2 (8-inch) round pans 2 (9-inch) round pans 2 (11 x 7-inch) baking dishes
1 (10-inch) springform pan	12 cups	1 (9-inch) tube pan 1 (10-inch) Bundt pan 2 (8-inch) round pans	2 (8 x 4-inch) loaf pans 2 (9-inch) round pans 2 (11 x 7-inch) baking dishes
2 (9-inch) round pans	12 cups	1 (9-inch) tube pan 1 (10-inch) Bundt pan 1 (10-inch) springform pan	2 (8-inch) round pans 2 (8 x 4-inch) loaf pans 2 (11 x 7-inch) baking dishes

PAN	CAPACITY	SUBSTITUTIONS	
1 (13 x 9 x 2-inch) baking dish	15 cups	1 (10-inch) Bundt pan 1 (15 x 10-inch) jelly-roll pan	2 (9-inch) round pans 3 (8-inch) round pans
1 (15 x 10 x 1-inch) jelly-roll pan or baking sheet	15 cups	1 (13 x 9-inch) baking dish 1 (10-inch) Bundt pan	2 (8-inch) round pans 2 (9-inch) round pans
1 (10-inch) tube pan	16 cups	2 (8-inch) square baking dishes 2 (9-inch) square baking dishes 2 (9-inch) deep-dish pie plates 2 (10-inch) pie plates	2 (9 x 5-inch) loaf pans 3 (9-inch) round pans 4 (8-inch) pie plates
2 (10-inch) round pans	22 cups	2 (10-inch) springform pans 3 or 4 (9-inch) round pans 5 (8-inch) round pans	

TABLE 11 Pan sizes (conventional and metric)

CONVENTIONAL MEASURE (INCHES)	METRIC MEASURE (CENTIMETERS)
8 x 2-inch round	20 x 5-centimeter round
8 x 4 x 3-inch loaf	20 x 11 x 7.5-centimeter loaf
8 x 8-inch square	20 x 20-centimeter square
9 x 2-inch round	22 x 5-centimeter round
9 x 5 x 3-inch loaf	22 x 12.5 x 7.5-centimeter loaf
9 x 9-inch square	22 x 22-centimeter square
10 x 4½-inch tube	25 x 11-centimeter tube
13 x 9-inch rectangle	33 x 23-centimeter rectangle
15 x 10-inch rectangle	38 x 25-centimeter rectangle
17 x 11-inch rectangle	43 x 28-centimeter rectangle

Equipment

See table 6 (page 23) for my top recommendations.

Baking pans. Baking pans come in a variety of shapes and sizes, including rectangular, square, loaf, and round, as well as those designed for muffins, doughnuts, and novelty shapes. Light-colored metal pans tend to produce a lighter crust, whereas dark metal pans tend to produce a darker crust and bake more quickly. Nonstick pans are often very dark and produce an uneven result. Glass pans can be used in place of metal pans. If you are using a dark or glass pan, decrease the oven temperature by 25 degrees. I highly recommend the pans sold at Williams-Sonoma, both in the traditional finish and Goldtouch Nonstick. They are made of commercial-grade aluminized steel, and the Goldtouch is light in color so the oven temperature doesn't need to be decreased.

Baking sheets. Also known as cookie sheets, baking sheets are flat, metal sheets designed for baking and roasting. As is the case for baking pans (see above), food bakes much more quickly on dark and nonstick baking sheets, so use them with care. I get the best results using aluminum baking sheets lined with parchment paper or a high-quality silicone baking mat (see below).

Cooling racks. Cooling racks are wire racks set on short legs. This design allows air to circulate around and under freshly baked goods as they cool. Different sizes are available; I prefer large, two-tier racks, which are useful when I bake multiple items.

Parchment paper. Parchment paper is used to line baking sheets to create a nonstick surface. It is disposable. An alternative is a silicone baking mat (see below).

Pastry bags. Pastry bags, or piping bags, are cone- or triangular-shaped bags made from cloth, paper, or plastic. When the bag is squeezed, the contents are forced through the tip. Pastry bags are handy for decorating cakes, cupcakes, and cookies. Make a homemade pastry bag by snipping a bottom corner off a large ziplock bag.

Pastry blender. A pastry blender is used to cut cold fat into dry ingredients when making crusts for bars and squares. This tool also is helpful for mashing soft ingredients, such as avocados and bananas.

Rolling pin. A rolling pin is a cylindrical kitchen tool used to flatten dough. There are two styles: roller-style pins, which have a thick roller with small handles on the ends, and rod, or French, rolling pins, which are thinner with tapered ends. Both kinds are usually made from wood, but glass, marble, silicone, and stainless steel rolling pins exist. I prefer to use a French-style wooden rolling pin.

Silicone baking mat. Reusable silicone baking mats are used to line baking sheets to form a nonstick surface. Unlike parchment paper, they can be used countless times, eliminate waste, are easy to clean, and are reasonably priced. I recommend Silpat brand. Most low-end versions don't work as well.

Spatula, silicone or rubber. A spatula is used for scraping mixing bowls, smoothing batter or dough, and folding ingredients together. Silicone or rubber spatulas are flexible, heat resistant, sturdy, and have smooth edges.

Ingredients and Food Terms

Agave nectar. See page 11.

Almond butter. Almond butter is a nut paste made from almonds. It is a slightly sweet and popular alternative to peanut butter. Almonds are high in good-for-you mono-unsaturated fats and an excellent source of calcium, fiber, magnesium, and vitamin E. To learn how to make homemade nut and seed butter, see sidebar, page 13.

Baking powder. See page 9.

Baking soda. See page 10.

Biscotti. Biscotti means "twice-baked" and refers to a long, often dry and hard cookie designed for dunking in coffee or tea. The dough is baked in a log form, then cooled, sliced, and returned to the oven to bake on low heat until crisp.

Buckwheat cereal, creamy. A great substitution for oats, creamy buckwheat cereal is made from stone-ground buckwheat groats and is a good source of protein and dietary fiber. I recommend using Bob's Red Mill Creamy Buckwheat.

Cashew butter. Smooth, creamy, and rich, cashew butter is a nut paste made from raw or roasted cashews. Cashews are a good source of calcium, protein, iron, B vitamins, and zinc.

Cocoa powder. There are two types of unsweetened cocoa powder: natural and Dutch-processed. See page 15 for more information.

Coconut, shredded dried. Shredded dried coconut is designed for baking and is typically sweetened. The recipes in this book are formulated with unsweetened finely shredded dried coconut, which is available at most natural foods stores. Let's Do . . . Organic by Edward & Sons makes an allergy-friendly variety.

Coconut milk. Coconut milk is a sweet, white liquid derived from the meat of a coconut. It isn't a dairy product. See pages 14 and 17 for more information.

Coconut oil. Coconut oil is extracted from the meat of a coconut. Because coconut oil is solid at room temperature, it isn't always possible to substitute other oils for coconut oil. Each recipe indicates if other oils can be used. See page 18 for more information.

Confectioners' sugar. See page 11.

Dough. Dough is an unbaked mass of ingredients that can be kneaded or rolled. It has a thicker consistency—and generally less fat, liquid, and sugar—than batter.

Flaxseeds. Flaxseeds are brown or golden seeds that contain soluble fiber, cancer-fighting lignans, and omega-3 fatty acids. In most instances, they should be ground before using; grind flaxseeds in a coffee grinder or purchase them in ground form (labeled "flax meal" or "flaxseed meal"). Store flaxseeds in the refrigerator or freezer.

Hempseeds. Hempseeds are highly nutritious seeds from the *Cannabis sativa* plant; however, they don't contain psychoactive properties. They are an excellent source of protein and have the optimal balance of omega-3 to omega-6 fatty acids.

Maple syrup, pure. See page 11.

Molasses. See page 11.

Nondairy milk. See pages 12 and 17.

Nut or seed butter. Nut butters are made from ground nuts, and seed butters are made from ground seeds (see Almond Butter, page 141, Cashew Butter, page 141, Peanut Butter, below, and Tahini, below). I recommend using natural, roasted varieties for the most flavor, with the only ingredient being the nut or seed itself. See page 12.

Peanut butter. Peanut butter is made from roasted peanuts that are ground to a paste. I recommend using organic peanut butter that doesn't contain any added oils or sugar.

Streusel. A crumbly mixture made of fat, flour, sugar, and often spices, streusel is used as a sweet, textured topping for baked goods, such as cakes and muffins. The term is derived from the German word *streuen*, which means to sprinkle or scatter.

Sugar. In baking, sugar not only sweetens but also adds color, tenderness, texture, and volume to baked goods and acts as a preservative. Sugar comes in many forms. For information about the sugar varieties used in this book, see pages 10 to 12.

Tahini. Tahini is a paste made from ground sesame seeds. It is typically used in Middle Eastern and Mediterranean cuisines and is somewhat bitter. Available either raw or roasted, tahini is a main ingredient in hummus but also adds a pleasant flavor to baked goods. Most versions are roasted unless otherwise indicated. See page 12 for more information.

Unrefined cane sugar. See page 11.

Vanilla. Vanilla, a popular flavoring, is sold as a bean in its whole form; in baking, vanilla extract is typically used. To make your own vanilla extract, cut a whole vanilla bean in half lengthwise and put it in ¾ cup of vodka. Seal and let steep for at least 6 months.

Zest. The zest is the colorful outer rind of citrus fruit. Rich in flavor, zest can be removed using a grater, knife, vegetable peeler, or zester. The white pith inside the zest is very bitter and should be avoided. I recommend Microplane graters.

Techniques

Beat. To beat a mixture is to use a spoon, wire whisk, or an electric mixer to stir with a brisk movement until the mixture is smooth. When using a stand mixer, use the paddle attachment.

Blend. To blend is to process two or more ingredients in a food processor or blender until smooth and uniform.

Boil. To boil is to heat water or other liquids in a saucepan over high heat until bubbles form, rising steadily and breaking the surface.

Cut in. To cut solid fats into dry ingredients when making dough for biscuits, pastries, or scones, use two knives, a pastry blender, your fingertips, or a food processor. Continue until the mixture resembles coarse crumbs.

Drizzle. To drizzle means to pour a thin stream of liquid, such as a glaze or melted chocolate, over baked goods, such as cakes, cookies, and bars.

Dust. To dust a food, pan, or work surface is to coat it lightly with cocoa powder, confectioners' sugar, or flour. For example, cocoa powder can be used to coat pans before chocolate cake batter is added. Confectioners' sugar is often dusted over finished desserts for aesthetic reasons and to impart a little extra sweetness. Flour is often used on work surfaces for rolling dough or inside an oiled pan to prevent sticking.

Grate. To grate a food item, use a wide box grater or the grating attachment of a food processor. Grated fruits and vegetables are sometimes used in baked goods, such as carrot cake. When the recipe indicates that a box grater, not a food processor, should be used, it's because some foods release excess moisture when grated in a food processor, which will make baked goods soggy.

Knead. To knead dough, work it with the heels of your hands, using a pressing and folding motion.

Mix. To mix is to stir two or more ingredients until they are evenly combined. Mixing can be done in a blender or food processor, with a mixer, or manually with a spoon and bowl.

Score. To score is to create shallow cuts in dough with a sharp knife.

Scrape down. To scrape down is to move a firm rubber or silicone spatula around the inside of a bowl, reincorporating any loose bits into the mixture. This method ensures all ingredients will be mixed thoroughly.

Sift. To sift is to use a sieve to break up clumps and aerate dry ingredients. Whisking is a suitable technique for sifting. Recipes can indicate whether to sift the ingredient before or after measuring. For the recipes in this book, measurements are given for dry ingredients *before* they are sifted.

Whisk. To whisk is to rapidly beat air into a moist mixture by using a wire whisk or electric mixer. Dry ingredients are often stirred with a whisk to combine them.

Other

Dash. A dash is a measurement equivalent to $\frac{1}{16}$ teaspoon.

Heaping. A heaping teaspoon, tablespoon, or cup means that it is slightly rounded beyond the standard capacity. Fill the measuring utensil slightly more than usual.

Pinch. A pinch is an inexact measurement that refers to using the thumb and forefinger to pick up a small amount of a dry ingredient. A pinch is equivalent to about $\frac{1}{16}$ teaspoon.

Scant. If a recipe calls for a scant teaspoon, tablespoon, cup, or other measurement, just barely fill the measuring spoon or cup.

SUPPLIERS

Here is a listing of retailers that sell gluten-free and allergy-friendly products. Because manufacturers change their formulations, be sure to always read labels, even on products that you've used many times before. In addition, try to keep tabs on companies and their manufacturing procedures to make sure they remain safe for your diet.

Bob's Red Mill   *bobsredmill.com*

Bob's Red Mill manufactures both gluten-free and gluten-containing baking aids, beans, flaxseeds, flour, and grains. Specially marked packages indicate products that were produced in dedicated gluten-free, casein-free facilities.

Free From Market
freefrommarket.com

Free From Market carries common and hard-to-find allergen-free products, including gluten-free, low-carbohydrate, low-protein, and vegan groceries, along with body and skin care, cleaners, supplements, and more. The company does not carry products with "may contain" labels or those that contain artificial sweeteners, dyes, or genetically modified organisms.

GlutenFree.com
glutenfree.com

GlutenFree.com has been catering to people with celiac disease and those with restricted diets since 1993. The website features a wide variety of baked goods, baking supplies, books, mixes, snacks, vitamins, and more.

The Gluten-Free Mall
glutenfreemall.com

The Gluten-Free Mall has offered online shopping since 1998 and carries a wide selection of casein-free, gluten-free, wheat-free, and other allergen-free foods and dietary products.

King Arthur Flour
kingarthurflour.com

America's oldest flour company, King Arthur Flour began manufacturing flour in 1790. The company manufactures a gluten-free multipurpose mix—which is also allergen-free and certified kosher—that is packed at a dedicated gluten-free facility.

Natural Candy Store
naturalcandystore.com

The Natural Candy Store carries the largest online selection of organic and natural candy available, including dye-free candy canes and all-natural sprinkles. All products are free of artificial colors, dyes, flavors, or sweeteners; they also have no preservatives or hydrogenated oils. Products are searchable by category, such as certified gluten-free, vegan, and organic.

Pangea Vegan Products
veganstore.com

Pangea is an online store that offers a comprehensive selection of high-quality, cruelty-free, nonanimal-derived products, including body care, books, food, clothing, DVDs, pet products, and more. Many items are gluten-free and allergy-friendly.

Vegan Essentials
veganessentials.com

Vegan Essentials is one of America's oldest cruelty-free online retailers. Vegan owned and operated, the company specializes in high-quality animal-free products, including gluten-free items.

RESOURCES

AUTISM AND ADHD

Autism Network for Dietary Intervention	autismndi.com
GFCF Diet Support Group	gfcfdiet.com

CELIAC DISEASE AND GLUTEN-FREE

Canadian Celiac Association	celiac.ca
Celiac.com	celiac.com
Celiac Disease Foundation	celiac.org
Celiac Sprue Association	csaceliacs.org
Glutenfreedom.net	glutenfreedom.net
Gluten-Free Living	glutenfreeliving.com
Gluten Intolerance Group	www.gluten.net

FOOD ALLERGIES

Allergic Living	allergicliving.com
Food Allergy & Anaphylaxis Network	www.foodallergy.org
Food Allergy Initiative	faiusa.org
Living Without	livingwithout.com

ABOUT THE AUTHOR

Laurie Sadowski's love of food began with her first bite of rice Pablum. At a young age, she was introduced to fruit trees and vegetable gardens; her chore was to fill pots with fresh-picked cherries and green beans. While pursuing a music degree, she became a food writer and sampled eclectic cuisine from top restaurants. Her creativity in the kitchen began when she was diagnosed with celiac disease. Soon after, she self-published a gluten-free, casein-free cookbook, *Mission in the Kitchen*.

The adoption of a vegan diet further fueled Laurie's foodie fire. After winning the vegetarian category in a national recipe competition and cook-off, she became a vegan food columnist for her local newspaper. Her love of food and health, combined with a passion for helping others, drove her to write a series gluten-free cookbooks that also addressed other common food allergies. *The Allergy-Free Cook Bakes Bread*, published in 2011, is the first book in the series. *The Allergy-Free Cook Bakes Cakes and Cookies* is the second.

Laurie lives in the Niagara region of Ontario, Canada, where she promotes healthful living as a certified personal trainer and nutrition and wellness specialist. Visit her at theallergyfreecook.com.

Index

Recipe titles appear in *italics*.

A

agave nectar, 141
A-Little-Bit-of-Everything Cookies, 92
allergies/allergens, 2–5
almond(s)
  Biscotti, Chocolate-, 131
  butter, 141
  Butter Surprises, Chocolate-, 84–85
  extract, 14
  in *Nutty and Crunchy No-Bake Bars*, 130
  Squares, Triple-, 114–15
apple
  Cake with Cider Sauce, Autumn, 52–53
  cider vinegar, 16
  Crumb Squares, 124–25
Armenian Nutmeg Cake, 56
Autumn Apple Cake with Cider Sauce, 52–53

B

baking pans/baking sheets, 140
baking powder/baking soda, 9–10, 141
Banana-Chai Cupcakes, 68–69
bar(s)
  baking, 109–10
  Canadian Nanaimo, 112–13
  Chocolate-Mint Nanaimo, 113
  Nutty and Crunchy No-Bake, 130
  Shortbread, Billionaire's, 122–23
beating, 143
Billionaire's Shortbread, 122–23
biscotti
  about, 141
  baking, 109–10
  Cashew Butter-Date, 134–35
  Chocolate-Almond, 131
  Hazelnut, 137

  Maple-Cinnamon, 132–33
Bit-of-Everything Cookies, A-Little-, 92
Blackberry Buttermilk Cake, Simple, 49
blending, 143
Blondies, Chocolate, Pecan, and Raspberry, 117
Blondies, Peanut Butter and Jam, 116
Blueberry Brunch Cake, Wild, 46–47
boiling, 143
Boston Cream Pie, 36–37
brownie(s)
  Icebox Cookies, 94
  Icebox Cookies, Mint-, 94
  No-Bake Chocolate-Cherry, 119
  No-Bake Frosted Mint, 119
  Rich and Fudgy, 118
  Topped with Chocolate Chip Cookie Dough, 120–21
Brunch Cake, Wild Blueberry, 46–47
buckwheat cereal, 141
Bundt Cake, Caramel-Macchiato, 32–33
Bundt Cake, Chocolate Chunk-Orange, 30–31
buttermilk
  Cake, Cranberry-Cinnamon, 49
  Cake, Simple Blackberry, 49
  vegan, 4, 17
butter(s)
  almond, 141
  Almond, Surprises, Chocolate-, 84–85
  cashew
    about, 141
    Cupcakes, 62–63
    -Date Biscotti, 134–35
  coconut, 13
  nut/seed, 12, 13, 142
  peanut
    about, 142

  consistency of, 35
  Cookies, Chocolate Chip-, 97
  Cookies, Really Good, 97
  Explosion, Chocolate, 34–35
  and Jam Blondies, 116
  substitutes for, 17–19

C

Cacao Nibs, Shortbread with Dried Cherries and, 100–101
cake(s). *See also* cupcakes; mini cakes
  Apple, with Cider Sauce, Autumn, 52–53
  baking, 26, 27
  Blackberry Buttermilk, Simple, 49
  Boston Cream Pie, 36–37
  Caramel-Macchiato Bundt, 32–33
  Carrot, with Coconut Cream Frosting, Loaded, 42–43
  chocolate
    Carrot, with Good-For-You Frosting, 44–45
    Chunk-Orange Bundt, 30–31
    Layer Cake, Triple-, 38–39
    Peanut-Butter Explosion, 34–35
  cooling/slicing/storing, 27–28
  Cranberry-Cinnamon Buttermilk, 49
  equipment for, 25
  frosting and filling, 28–29
  Fruit and Nut, Festive, 54
  ingredients, 25
  measuring for, 27
  mixing & matching, 29
  Nutmeg, Armenian, 56
  Orange-Olive Oil, 48
  Pumpkin, with Cranberry Filling and Pecan Streusel, 40–41
  Short- , New Old-Fashioned Strawberry, 50–51
  Tahinopita, Greek, 55
  Wild Blueberry Brunch, 46–47
Canadian Nanaimo Bars, 112–13

Candy Cane Snowballs, Holiday, 86
Cane Snowballs, Holiday Candy, 86
Caramel-Macchiato Bundt Cake, 32–33
Cardamom Upside-Down Cakes, Individual Pear-, 79
Carrot Cake with Coconut Cream Frosting, Loaded, 42–43
Carrot Cake with Good-For-You Frosting, 44–45
casein
  on food labels, 4
  removal from diet, vi
cashew butter
  about, 141
  consistency of, 63
  Cupcakes, 62–63
  -Date Biscotti, 134–35
celiac disease, 1–2
cereal
  about, 141
  types of, 15
Chai Cupcakes, Banana-, 68–69
cherry(ies)
  Brownies, No-Bake Chocolate-, 119
  and Cacao Nibs, Shortbread with Dried, 100–101
  Cupcakes, Two-Bite Chocolate-Covered, 74–75
chip
  Cookie Dough, Brownies Topped with Chocolate, 120–21
  Cookies, Essential Chocolate, 88
  -Peanut Butter Cookies, Chocolate, 97
chocolate
  -Almond Biscotti, 131
  -Almond Butter Surprises, 84–85
  in *Boston Cream Pie*, 36–37
  brownie(s)
    Icebox Cookies, 94
    Icebox Cookies, Mint-, 94
    No-Bake, -Cherry, 119
    No-Bake Frosted Mint, 119
    Rich and Fudgy, 118
    Topped with Chocolate Chip Cookie Dough, 120–21
  in *Canadian Nanaimo Bars*, 112–13
  Carrot Cake with Good-For-You Frosting, 44–45

chip(s)
  Cookie Dough, Brownies Topped with, 120–21
  Cookies, Essential, 89
  as ingredient, 16
  -Peanut Butter Cookies, 97
Chunk-Orange Bundt Cake, 30–31
Chunk-Tahini Cookies, 88
cocoa (cacao)
  as ingredient, 15, 16
  Nibs, Shortbread with Dried Cherries and, 100–101
  powder, 15–16, 141
  -Coconut-Walnut Squares, 111
  Cookies with Raisins, Double-, 96
cupcakes
  with Chocolate Frosting, 64
  with Chocolate-Macadamia Frosting, 64
  Two-Bite, -Covered Cherry, 74–75
extract, 14
Frosting, Chocolate Cupcakes with, 64
-Hazelnut-Raspberry Thumbprints, 98–99
as ingredient, 15–16
Layer Cake, Triple-, 38–39
-Macadamia Frosting, Chocolate Cupcakes with, 64
-Mint Nanaimo Bars, 113
-Peanut Butter Explosion, 34–35
Pecan, and Raspberry Blondies, 117
Sandwich Cookies, Noreos, 102–3
Sauce, Sticky Date Cupcakes with Toffee, 72–73
topping, 123
Chunk-Orange Bundt Cake, Chocolate, 30–31
Chunk-Tahini Cookies, Chocolate, 88
Cider Sauce, Autumn Apple Cake with, 52–53
cider vinegar, 16
Cinnamon Biscotti, Maple-, 132–33
Cinnamon Buttermilk Cake, Cranberry-, 49
cocoa (cacao)
  about, 15
  Nibs, Shortbread with Dried Cherries and, 100–101
  powder, 15–16, 141

coconut
  about, 141
  in *Canadian Nanaimo Bars*, 112–13
  Cream Frosting, Loaded Carrot Cake with, 42–43
  Cupcakes, Mini Triple-, 78
  extract, 14
  as ingredient, 13–14
  milk, 14, 17, 141
  oil, 18, 141
  -Walnut Squares, 111
  -Walnut Squares, Chocolate-, 111
coffee
  in cakes, 32–33, 38–39
  in cookies, 94
  in cupcakes, 64
  French press for making, 39
  in squares, 118
  Starbucks, 33
confectioners' sugar, 141
conversions, 137–39
cookie(s)
  about, 81–83
  A-Little-Bit-of-Everything, 92
  chocolate
    -Almond Butter Surprises, 84–85
    Brownie Icebox, 94
    Brownie Icebox, Mint-, 94
    Chip, Dough, Brownies Topped with, 120–21
    Chip, Essential, 89
    Chunk-Tahini, 88
    Double-, with Raisins, 96
    -Hazelnut-Raspberry Thumbprints, 98–99
    Sandwich, Noreos, 102–3
  Gingerbread Men, Traditional, 106–7
  Holiday Candy Cane Snowballs, 86
  Ice-Cream Sandwiches, Nondairy, 97
  Macadamia, Double-, 90–91
  Maple Leaf, Cream-Filled, 104–5
  Mexican Wedding, 87
  Noatmeal Raisin, 95
  Orange Spice, 93
  Peanut Butter, Really Good, 97
  Shortbread with Dried Cherries and Cacao Nibs, 100–101
cooling racks, 140
corn
  as allergen, 2

removal from recipes, 3
xanthan gum made from, 9
*Cranberry-Cinnamon Buttermilk
  Cake,* 49
*Cranberry Filling and Pecan Streusel,
  Pumpkin Cake with,* 40–41
cream
  -Filled Maple Leaf Cookies, 104–5
  *Frosting, Loaded Carrot Cake with
    Coconut,* 42–43
  Pie, Boston, 36–37
cross-contamination, 5
*Crumble, Pumpkin Pie Squares with
  Pecan,* 126–27
Crumb Squares, Apple, 124–25
Crunchy No-Bake Bars, Nutty and, 139
cupcakes
  baking, 59, 60
  Banana-Chai, 68–69
  Cashew Butter, 62–63
  chocolate
    with Chocolate Frosting, 64
    *with Chocolate-Macadamia
      Frosting,* 64
    -Covered Cherry, Two-Bite, 74–75
  Coconut, Mini Triple-, 78
  *Date, with Toffee Chocolate Sauce,
    Sticky,* 72–73
  French Toast, 70–71
  Orange-Pineapple, 65
  *Strawberry-Vanilla, with Bakery-
    Style White Frosting,* 67
  Strawberry-Vanilla Glazed, 66–67
cutting in, 143

D
dairy products
  on food labels, 4, 5
  removal from diet/recipes, vi, 3
  substitutes for, 17–19
dash (measure), 144
date
  Biscotti, Cashew Butter-, 134–35
  *Cupcakes with Toffee Chocolate
    Sauce, Sticky,* 72–73
  and Pear Squares, Glazed, 128–29
*Double-Chocolate Cookies with
  Raisins,* 96
Double-Macadamia Cookies, 90–91
dough
  about, 20–21, 142

*Brownies Topped with Chocolate
  Chip Cookie,* 120–21
coconut oil and, 19
cookie, 81–82, 83
equipment for, 21, 23, 140–41
gluten for, 1
leavening in, 9
salt in, 15
techniques for, 143
*Dried Cherries and Cacao Nibs,
  Shortbread with,* 100–101
dried fruits, sulfites in, 3
drizzling, 143
dusting, 143

E
eggs
  as allergen, 3
  on food labels, 4, 5
  substitutes for, 13, 14, 19, 20
equipment for baking, 21, 140–43
Essential Chocolate Chip Cookies, 89
Everything Cookies, A-Little-Bit-of-, 92
Explosion, Chocolate-Peanut Butter,
  34–35
extracts, 14

F
fats, 12
Festive Fruit and Nut Cake, 54
Filled Maple Leaf Cookies, Cream-,
  104–5
*Filling and Pecan Streusel, Pumpkin
  Cake with Cranberry,* 40–41
flaxseeds, 142
flours
  substitutions for, 9
  types of, 2, 7–8
food allergies
  author and, vi
  common, 2–4, 16
food labels, 4–5
French coffee press, 39
French Toast Cupcakes, 70–71
frosted/frosting(s)
  *Chocolate Carrot Cake with Good-
    For-You,* 44–45
  Chocolate Cupcakes with Chocolate,
    64
  *Loaded Carrot Cake with Coconut
    Cream,* 42–43

Mint Brownies, No-Bake, 119
techniques for, 28, 61–62
fruit(s)
  dried, sulfites in, 3
  and fruit purées, 14
  and Nut Cake, Festive, 54
Fudgy Brownies, Rich and, 118

G
Gingerbread Men, Traditional, 106–7
Glazed Cupcakes, Strawberry-Vanilla,
  66–67
Glazed Date and Pear Squares, 128–29
gluten
  about, 1–2
  as allergen, 3
  author and, vi–vii
  cross-contamination and, 5
  hidden sources of, 5
*Good-For-You Frosting, Chocolate
  Carrot Cake with,* 44–45
Good Peanut Butter Cookies, Really, 97
grains
  as allergen, 2
  removal from recipes, 3
grating, 143
Greek Tahinopita, 55
guar gum, 9

H
Hazelnut Biscotti, 137
*Hazelnut-Raspberry Thumbprints,
  Chocolate-,* 98–99
heaping (measure), 144
hempseeds, 142
Holiday Candy Cane Snowballs, 86

I
Icebox Cookies, Brownie or *Mint
  Brownie,* 94
Ice-Cream Sandwiches, Nondairy, 97
*Individual Pear-Cardamom Upside-
  Down Cakes,* 79
ingredients for baking/pantry
  cereal, 15
  cider vinegar, 16
  cocoa/chocolate, 15–16
  coconut, 13–14
  extracts, 14
  fats, 12
  flours & starches, 6–9

food terms and, 141–43
fruit/fruit purées, 14
leavening, 9–10
nondairy milks, 12
nuts & seeds, 12–13
salt, 15
spices, 14
sweeteners, 10–12
techniques for, 21
xanthan gum, 9

J

Jam Blondies, Peanut Butter and, 116

K

kneading, 143

L

Layer Cake, Triple-Chocolate, 38–39
Leaf Cookies, Cream-Filled Maple-,
    104–5
leavening, 9–10
legumes
    as allergen, 2
    guar gum made from, 9
    removal from recipes, 3
lemon
    extract, 14
    in *New Old-Fashioned Strawberry
        Shortcake,* 50–51
    zest, 14
Little-Bit-of-Everything Cookies, A-, 92
*Loaded Carrot Cake with Coconut
    Cream Frosting,* 42–43

M

Macadamia Cookies, Double-, 90–91
Macchiato Bundt Cake, Caramel-,
    32–33
maple
    -*Cinnamon Biscotti,* 132–33
    extract, 14
    Leaf Cookies, Cream-Filled, 104–5
    syrup, 142
Men, Traditional Gingerbread, 106–7
Mexican Wedding Cookies, 87
milk protein, removal from diet, vi
milks, nondairy
    about, 142
    as ingredient, 12
    types of, 17

mini cakes
    *Individual Pear-Cardamom Upside-
        Down,* 79
    *Molten Lava, with Raspberry
        Sauce,* 76–77
    tips for making/frosting, 60–61
Mini Triple-Coconut Cupcakes, 78
mint
    -*Brownie Icebox Cookies,* 94
    Brownies, No-Bake Frosted, 119
    extract, 14
    Nanaimo Bars, Chocolate-Mint,
        113
mixing, 143
molasses, 142
*Molten Lava Mini Cakes with
    Raspberry Sauce,* 76–77

N

Nanaimo Bars, Canadian, 112–13
Nanaimo Bars, Chocolate-Mint, 113
*New Old-Fashioned Strawberry
    Shortcake,* 50–51
*Nibs, Shortbread with Dried Cherries
    and Cacao,* 100–101
nightshades, sensitivity to, 3
Noatmeal Raisin Cookies, 95
no-bake
    Bars, Nutty and Crunchy, 139
    Chocolate-Cherry Brownies, 119
    Frosted Mint Brownies, 119
nondairy milk(s)
    about, 142
    as ingredient, 12
    Ice-Cream Sandwiches, 97
    types of, 17
Noreos Chocolate Sandwich Cookies,
    102–3
Nutmeg Cake, Armenian, 56
nut(s). *See also* specific types of
    as allergen, 2
    Bars, Nutty and Crunchy No-Bake,
        130
    butter, 12, 13, 142
    Cake, Festive Fruit and, 54
    as ingredient, 12, 13
    milk, 17
    removal from recipes, 3

O

oats, 5

*Old-Fashioned Strawberry Shortcake,
    New,* 50–51
Olive Oil Cake, Orange-, 48
orange
    Bundt Cake, Chocolate Chunk-,
        30–31
    drizzle, 129
    -*Olive Oil Cake,* 48
    -*Pineapple Cupcakes,* 65
    Spice Cookies, 93
    zest, 14

P

pan sizes, 137–39
parchment paper, 140
pastry bags, 140
pastry blender, 140
peanut(s)
    as allergen, 2
    butter(s)
        about, 142
        consistency of, 35
        Cookies, Chocolate Chip-, 97
        Cookies, Really Good, 97
        Explosion, Chocolate-, 34–35
        *Ice-Cream Sandwiches, Non-
            dairy,* 97
        and Jam Blondies, 116
    removal from recipes, 3
*Pear-Cardamom Upside-Down Cakes,
    Individual,* 79
Pear Squares, Glazed Date and, 128–29
pecan(s)
    *Crumble, Pumpkin Pie Squares
        with,* 126–27
    in *Nutty and Crunchy No-Bake
        Bars,* 130
    and Raspberry Blondies, Chocolate,
        117
    *Streusel, Pumpkin Cake with Cran-
        berry Filling and,* 40–41
Pie, Boston Cream, 36–37
*Pie Squares with Pecan Crumble,
    Pumpkin,* 126–27
pinch (measure), 144
pineapple, in *Loaded Carrot Cake with
    Coconut Cream Frosting,* 42–43
Pineapple Cupcakes, Orange-, 65
pseudograins, 3
*Pumpkin Cake with Cranberry Filling
    and Pecan Streusel,* 40–41

Pumpkin Pie Squares with Pecan Crumble, 126–27

R

Raisin Cookies, Noatmeal, 95
Raisins, Double-Chocolate Cookies with, 96
raspberry
    Blondies, Chocolate, Pecan, and, 117
    Sauce, Molten Lava Mini Cakes with, 76–77
    Thumbprints, Chocolate-Hazelnut-, 98–99
Really Good Peanut Butter Cookies, 97
Rich and Fudgy Brownies, 118
rolling pin, 140

S

salt, 15
Sandwich Cookies, Noreos Chocolate, 102–3
Sauce, Autumn Apple Cake with Cider, 52–53
Sauce, Molten Lava Mini Cakes with Raspberry, 76–77
scant (measure), 144
scoring, 143
scraping down, 144
seed(s)
    as allergen, 2
    butter, 12, 13, 142
    as ingredient, 12, 13
    milk, 17
    removal from recipes, 3
Shortbread, Billionaire's, 122–23
Shortbread with Dried Cherries and Cacao Nibs, 100–101
Shortcake, New Old-Fashioned Strawberry, 50–51
sifting, 144
silicone baking mat, 140–41
Simple Blackberry Buttermilk Cake, 49
Snowballs, Holiday Candy Cane, 86
soy
    as allergen, 3
    on food labels, 4, 5
    milk, 17
    substitutes for, 19
spatula, 141

Spice Cookies, Orange, 93
spices, 14
square(s), 109–10
    Almond, Triple-, 114–15
    Apple Crumb, 124–25
    brownies
        No-Bake Frosted Mint, 119
        Rich and Fudgy, 118
        Topped with Chocolate Chip Cookie Dough, 120–21
    Chocolate, Pecan, and Raspberry Blondies, 117
    Chocolate-Coconut-Walnut, 111
    Coconut-Walnut, 111
    Date and Pear, Glazed, 128–29
    Peanut Butter and Jam Blondies, 116
    Pumpkin Pie, with Pecan Crumble, 126–27
Starbucks coffee, 33
starches and flours, 6–9
Sticky Date Cupcakes with Toffee Chocolate Sauce, 72–73
storing foods, 22–23
strawberry
    Shortcake, New Old-Fashioned, 50–51
    -Vanilla Cupcakes with Bakery-Style Frosting, 67
    -Vanilla Glazed Cupcakes, 66–67
streusel, 142
Streusel, Pumpkin Cake with Cranberry Filling and Pecan, 40–41
sugar, 142
sulfites, sensitivity to, 3
super seeds, 13
suppliers, 144–45
Surprises, Chocolate-Almond Butter, 84–85
sweeteners, 10–12

T

tahini
    about, 142
    Cookies, Chocolate Chunk-, 88
    Tahinopita, Greek, 55
techniques for baking, 21–22, 143–44
Thumbprints, Chocolate-Hazelnut-Raspberry, 98–99
toasting nuts/seeds/coconut, 13
Toffee Chocolate Sauce, Sticky Date Cupcakes with, 72–73

tools for baking, 23
Traditional Gingerbread Men, 106–7
triple
    -Almond Squares, 114–15
    -Chocolate Layer Cake, 38–39
    -Coconut Cupcakes, Mini, 78
Two-Bite Chocolate-Covered Cherry Cupcakes, 74–75

U

unrefined cane sugar, 142
Upside-Down Cakes, Individual Pear-Cardamom, 79

V

vanilla
    about, 142–43
    Cupcakes with Bakery-Style White Frosting, Strawberry-, 67
    extract, 14
    Glazed Cupcakes, Strawberry-, 66–67
vegan buttermilk, 17

W

walnut(s)
    in Nutty and Crunchy No-Bake Bars, 130
    Squares, Chocolate-Coconut-, 111
    Squares, Coconut-, 111
Wedding Cookies, Mexican, 87
wheat
    as allergen, 3
    on food labels, 4
whisking, 144
White Frosting, Strawberry-Vanilla Cupcakes with Bakery-Style, 67
whole foods, in diet, vi, vii
Wild Blueberry Brunch Cake, 46–47

X

xanthan gum, 9

Y

yeast
    as allergen, 2
    dough, 20–21
    removal from recipes, 4

Z

zest, 143

Book Publishing Co.

books that educate, inspire, and empower

To find your favorite vegetarian products online, visit:
healthy-eating.com

The Allergy-Free Cook Bakes Bread
Laurie Sadowski
978-1-57067-262-0 • $14.95

Simple Treats
Ellen Abraham
978-1-57067-137-1 • $14.95

Gluten-Free Gourmet Desserts and Baked Goods
Valerie Cupillard
978-1-57067-187-6 • $24.95

Food Allergies
*Jo Stepaniak, MSEd,
Vesanto Melina, MS, RD, and
Dina Aronson, RD*
978-1-55312-046-9 • $11.95

Food Allergy Survival Guide
*Vesanto Melina, RD,
Jo Stepaniak, MSEd, and
Dina Aronson, RD*
978-1-57067-163-0 • $19.95

Purchase these health titles and cookbooks from your local bookstore or natural food store,
or you can buy them directly from:

Book Publishing Company • P.O. Box 99 • Summertown, TN 38483 • 1-800-695-2241

Please include $3.95 per book for shipping and handling.